A HISTORY OF Virgin RECORDS

CONTRIBUTORS

RICHARD BRANSON

Founder of Virgin Records
Chairman of Virgin

SIMON DRAPER

Co-founder of Virgin Records
Chairman of Palawan Press Ltd.

KEN BERRY

Chairman & CEO of Virgin Music Group Worldwide
President and CEO of EMI Music Group International

TERRY SOUTHERN

Screenwriting credits include
Dr. Strangelove, Easy Rider, Barbarella;
Novels include
The Magic Christian, Candy, Blue Movie.
Anthology of Short Stories entitled Red Dirt Marijuana & Other Tastes,
Further Numerous Short Stories, Articles, Essays
and is also currentlyteaching at Columbia & Yale UniversitiEs.

FOR INFORMATION,
address:

Sisterhood Farm,
Cloakham Drive,
Axminster, Devon, England EX 13

PB ISBN #: 1-89911600-1
HB ISBN #: 1-89911605-2

Origination by Panorama Inc.
Further origination, printing and binding by Mandarin U.K. Ltd, (a division of the Reed/Elsevier Plc Group)

A HISTORY OF Virgin RECORDS

by:

Terry Southern

with

Richard Branson

Simon Draper

Ken Berry

Edited and compiled
by:

Perry Richardson

Art Direction and Design
by:

Marc Balet
with
Darrin Ehardt
and
Marlon Richards

Additional editorial and design research by:
Tony Lacey, Coco Godebska, Chelita Salvatori, Saida Anwar, Adam Richardson,
Gawain Rainey, David Webb, Julian Brown, Rose Rainey, Dusanka Srvic, & Janet-Elen Richardson

Copy Editing and Proofreading:
Patty Romanowski

Project Co-ordinators for Virgin Records:
Jeremy Silver, Lisa Anderson, Andy Dowsett

A C K N O W L E D G E M E N T S

The list of acknowledgements pertaining to this job o' work could well make the lengthiest and most tear-stained Oscar acceptance speech appear terse by comparison. However, brooking no argument, the publisher would at least like to especially thank the following characters for all of their help in making this book possible:

Chris Kewbank, Catherine Turner, Nancy Berry, Paul Conroy, Ray Cooper, Steve Pritchard, Simon Hopkins, Dave Boyd, Ken Marshall, Amber Ross, Pennie Pike, Emma Donna, Jenny Goodwyn-Marks, Jayne Jones, Chips Chipperfield, Bob Smeaton, Jeremy Lascelles, Margaret Van Sicklen, Sarah Duffy, Ritsa Galitsis, Naomi Taubleb, Ethel Manibo, Carey Fox, Rick Albert, Nancy Grome, Chris Whoerle, Juliette Mann, David Enthoven, Keri Maundrell, Fujiko, Gail Gerber, Edward Richardson, James Richardson, Anita Pallenberg, Earl McGrath, Bobby Zarem, Vera Santo Domingo, John & Aglaë Seilern, Sandro & Charuvan Sursock, Charles O'Donnell, Emanuele di Savoia, Alejandra de Andia, Richard Charkin, David Macmillan, Ivan Gillett, Charlie Gillett, Robbie Montgomery, Dede Miller, Vicky Fox, Jane Rose, Sherry Daly, Nancy Benson, Angelica Torn, John Torn, Gordon & Barbera Rosen, Brenda Richardson, Pat & Fred Ferris, Tony Ferris, John & Ruth York, Steve Black, Brenda Burt, Michelle Slee, Mike & Jackie Curle, Arlene Tarte, Tim Linn, Rowley Weller, Trevor Key, Brian Cooke, Andre Csillag, William Claxton, Gered Markowitz, Anton Corbijn, Bob Gruen, Per Gustafsson, Steve Double, Sheila Rock, Peter Anderson, Liz Carselake, Jak Kilby, Simon Fowler, Dennis Morriss, Adrian Boot, Stephanie Pfriender & each of the photographers involved together with their assistants, the magazines & newspapers accredited & other journals both in the U.k. & abroad that have proved to be invaluable reference sources, as well as everyone at Virgin, Hut Records, Palawan Press, The Special Photographers Company, Balet & Albert, Initial Films & T.V. , Zarem Inc., Laister Dickson, Real World, Partridge & Story, Redferns, All Action, Retna, Sonicon Ltd., Panorama Inc., Mandarin Offset Ltd., & last but not least of course, a special tribute has surely to go to

"THE GREAT WESTERN OUTFIT."

PUBLISHER'S NOTE

Let me tell you, life is not all a bed of roses in the publishing game. My partner, one Julio Santo Domingo, suggests with grim relish that we have, and I quote, "surely cooled out any possible rumble with the Ayatollah." Personally, I feel that – like the Pope – we have produced a lasting tome, free from pretension and blessed with a soupçon of the miraculous *je ne sais quoi* to lube its chart-topping destiny.

It's been brought to my attention, however, that a certain amount of confusion might possibly still arise due to the super-abundance (albeit star-studded! Ed.) of contributors. In order to establish clarity, therefore (Will you get on with it? Ed.), I would like to make the following declaration: The main body of text has, of course, been written by the great Terry Southern, and all other text accredited to the relevant contributor – Richard Branson (R.B.), Simon Draper (S.D.), Ken Berry (K.B.) – and quotes from musicians and reviews credited accordingly. (As if we couldn't work that out on our own. Damnation! *J'accuse!* Ed.)

PERRY RICHARDSON

INTRODUCTION

by TERRY SOUTHERN

It was the winter of '72, and I had just survived the Stones' American tour. Despite the mega-vitamin and "ultra-energizer" regime strictly administered by tour physician, Dr. Stan E. Ellis (the celebrated biochemist from California), I felt completely exhausted and in a state of near remorse at having accepted a publisher's commission to research and write a brief history of The Early Rock Years. I knew my best bet for a quick info-fix would be to find Mr. Simon Draper, who, even at this early date, had gained a know-it-all rep and the heavyweight nick name of **"The Maven of Swing Street."** My several attempts to find him at his offices in Harley Street ("to be near a decent croaker just in case" was how he explained it) were to no avail. "Oh, he's always on the go," I was informed by his bevy of assistants, **"ferreting out fresh talent."** And that was how I did eventually discover him, just departing a club in one of the mean byways off Wardour Street, where he had been listening to ("auditioning" is perhaps more apt. Ed.) a young group who called themselves The Crud (a.k.a. The Bloody Crud, and later The Right Bloody Crud, circa '72, waterfront buskers from the Scapa Flow environs, Ed.). As I neared the end of the street, if indeed, such a sinister cobble path may be so termed, I heard a few open-fret riffs drifting towards me, and at the same time made out the figure of Simon Draper directly ahead. After a brief introduction, I ventured a remark which I hoped would serve to identify me as one who was no stranger to the world of rock. "Sounds like they're really cooking in there," I said genially.

Draper put his head to one side and fixed me with a formulative gaze. "It's curiously appropriate," he said, "that you should use a culinary metaphor, but I'm very much afraid it's a bit of tripe gone off the boil." Then he added with a twinkle, "If you discern my implication."Although I was not familiar with that particular and uniquely British phrase, there was no mistaking its meaning (I should think not! Ed.), so I was spared the ordeal of hearing the early Crud. My meeting with Simon Draper, however, served me in very good stead indeed. He proved to be an invaluable source of Rock savvy and info over the winter months to come while I forged ahead with my Early Rock Years opus. It should come as no suprise then that I would feel only too delighted to provide objective commentary (we've got a rudd hope, Ed.) regarding the extraordinary Virgin birth and ascension which he of course so adroitly fathered for

'lo on twenty-one illustrious years.

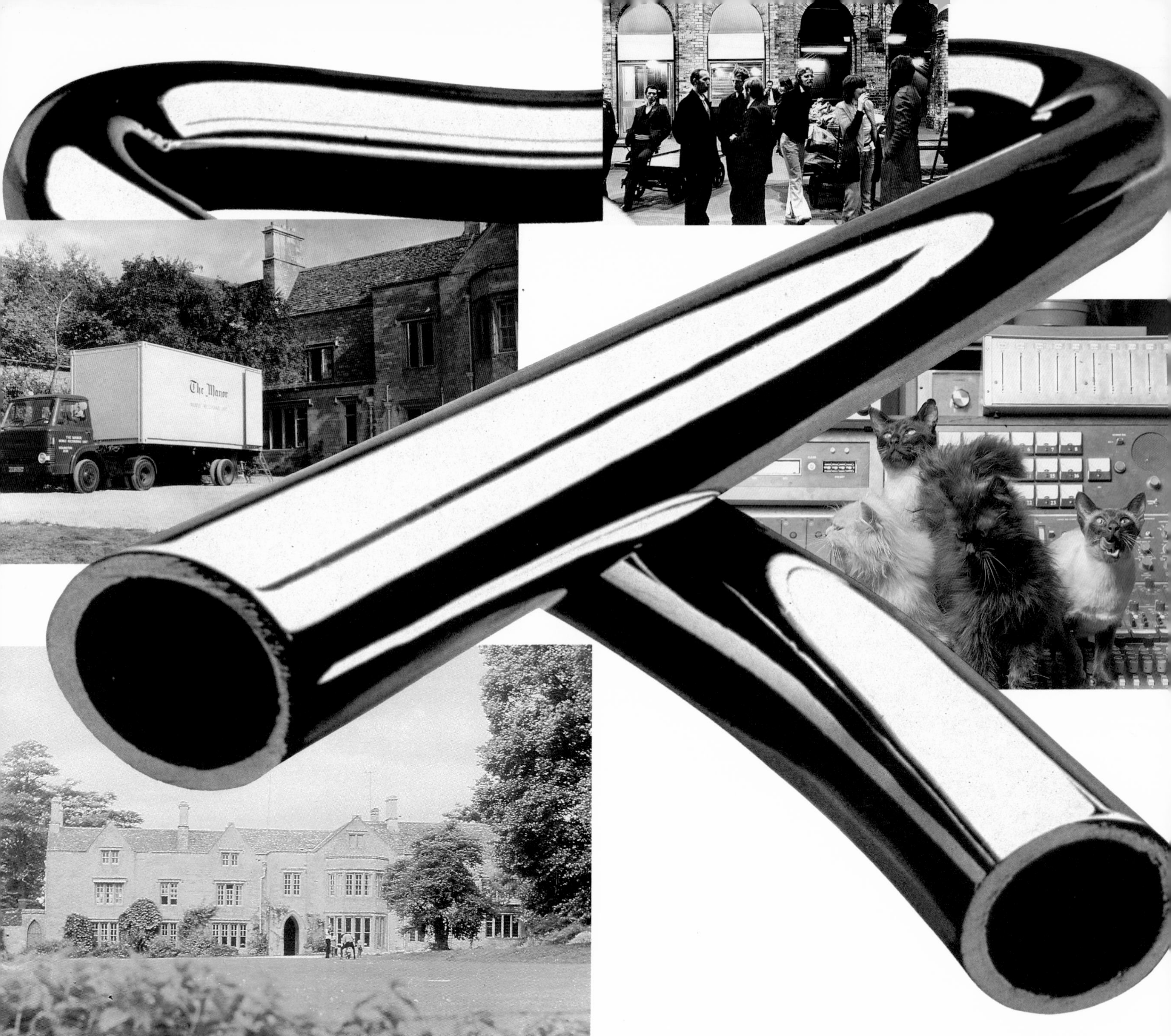

"I saw a tiny advertisement for a beautiful little castle in Wales, with a nice spiral turret, for £ 2,000 and thought, Wouldn't it be pleasant for rock bands to actually record in the country rather than checking in and checking out of London? So I went to see this castle and discovered that it was slap dab in the middle of a housing estate – they'd rather forgotten to mention that in the details. Then on the way back to London my car broke down literally just beside the drive that leads up to the manor. So I walked up this little lane, climbed over the wall, and there was this beautiful old fallen-down country house, and I just thought, This is it, this is the place – then managed somehow to borrow the money to buy it and create a studio." R. B.

"I only knew Virgin through buying records at their shops, but I had a friend of mine who was driving an old London taxi for them, taking boxes of records to railway stations for delivery by Red Star to stores outside of London. He said that there was a job going at Virgin, was I interested, and that was my introduction. I worked as an accounts clerk above the Notting Hill Gate shop. Simon was very much in charge of all the music – it was almost entirely his concept. He'd been acting as the buyer for the retail chain before taking over the formation of the record company, and I guess it was his musical vision that determined the direction Virgin took. I think one of Richard's great strengths is that he's prepared to back people, he had total confidence in Simon which, of course, proved to be well founded. I don't think anyone really knew at that time, however, whether Virgin was going to last or not. We were all quite young – I was twenty, Richard I think was twenty-one, Simon was twenty one, and everyone was doing it just because it was there, it was fun, it was a great thing to do." K.B.

"I'd met up in London with my second cousin, Richard Branson, whose real interest was in having started a magazine, out of which as a sideline to begin with, had come the mail order company, which developed rapidly on an international basis. Next came the first shops, **the Manor,** and then I started the record company at the back of the mail order headquarters, which was above the shop in Notting Hill Gate. I had this wonderful opportunity: Richard had asked me to start this label without really knowing what I was going to do, no one else really questioned what I was up to. The direction to take initially was fairly clearly indicated by the demand we were getting through the retail and mail order company, so in the **summer of '73** we launched the label with four records: *Tubular Bells*, Gong's *The Flying Teapot*, *Manor Live* (made up of a bunch of friends, including Elkie Brooks and Robert Palmer jamming together), and *The Faust Tapes*, by a German group called Faust, who'd already had three albums out and were a very important signing for us at the time. We managed to use a work by the artist Bridget Reilly for the cover, and then the big gimmick was that the album was released for the price of a single, which of course meant it sold extremely well – something like 100,000 copies. But then ***Tubular Bells*** had also begun to make its mark!" S.D.

You will probably have discovered by now from Music Week or your Island and EMI rep that we are about to launch our own independent label. We thought that we would let you know clearly what will be happening with our label before you get snowed under by all the leaflets, brochures and general publicity that the reps will thrust upon you.

Naturally, we shall be doing our best to promote and publicise our records. As retailers ourselves, however, we have often been painfully reminded that even the best publicised records are not fully backed by a grass-roots sales service. We are confident that Island's excellent distribution, backed up by EMI, will get you the records you want. But, if by chance, you're having difficulties, or just want more information, please get in touch with us direct, by phone or letter, and tell us your problems.

In case this is the first thing you've heard about the label, we shall be releasing four albums on May 25th: Mick Oldfield's Tubular Bells V2001; Gong's Radio Gnome Part 1.The Flying Teapot V2002; Steve York's Camelo Pardalis V2003, all at a recommended price of £2.19 (with the price structure of a normal Island ILPS album). The fourth album, Faust Tapes by Faust VC501, will be selling for 48p, but your mark-up will stay at 33 1/3%. In any event, you can get all the immediately relevant details from your rep.

Yours faithfully,

Richard Branson

VIRGIN RECORDS, 130 NOTTING HILL GATE, LONDON W11 TELEPHONES: 01-229 8131/3206

DEREK AND CLIVE COME AGAIN:

WARNING

The **CLEAN UP NOXIOUS TRASH** Association has been specially formed to oppose and, if possible, prevent the release of this obnoxious and filthy gramophone record.

– ONANISM – CANCER – EXCRETION – A FAMOUS FILM ACTRESS NOW DECEASED – INCEST – FELLATIO – COUGHING – ALFIE NOAKES – PUBLIC LAVATORIES – SPONTANEOUS VERSIFICATION –

– these are the things what Derek and Clive 'got into' since they became famous. We warn you again:

THIS RECORD IS NOT FUNNY! IT IS MERELY OBSCENE!

Out on Virgin Records. Album V2094. Cassette TCV2094.

"John Varnom was not vital to Virgin's success but he did write a lot of the crazy adverts and campaigns through those early years. He'd come up with pastiches of ads and even of journalists of the day – so that if the original was at all pompous his send-ups were funny because they were so accurate. Richard had, I think, a kind of love/hate relationship with him, because John did have a tendency toward sabotaging all he'd built, suddenly deciding to blow it all up and us along with it!"

S.D.

"Roger Dean designed and made this logo. There was a lovely Australian girl we knew at the time who we got to be the model. I kept in touch with her for years. She's got about five children now and lives in Australia – she was delightful."

R.B.

"Caroline was our export company. We were going to print the label and make the record so that you had to *break the virgin in* every time you put it on – and have a red inner lining to each sleeve!"

R.B.

"Simon had asked Trevor Key to come up with a new logo for us, which we agreed would be in the form of a signature. Trevor then found a graphic designer by the name of Ray Kite to simply write out the name in every variation of style imaginable. I remember discussing all of this at Virgin and as we were talking, this guy got up from the table to go to the loo, looked over his shoulder, and just scribbled the now-famous Virgin logo on a piece of paper

– then he went off and sent us a bill for it"

R.B.

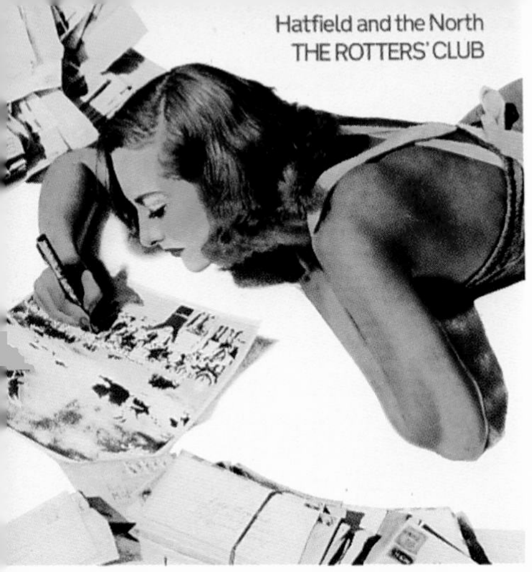

THE EARLY SEVENTIES

HENRY COW

"The caption to Tangerine Dream's first album was mine – 'Music That Melts.' We used to sit there and have these brainstorming sessions and I remember vividly having this idea because of Salvador Dali's soft watches, but then Trevor (Key) went off and set fire to dozens of records – the studio was literally littered with all of these melting records. He finally caught the shot, and the finished poster was this melting album dripping blobs of vinyl. It turned out to be a very successful ad campaign."
S.D.

"What I like about the records from the '70s is that they've got character. We were consciously trying to come up with things that were original and idiosyncratic, but it's astounding how much of it has either been reissued recently or has simply always remained in the catalogue."
S.D.

In the annals of rock and roll, the **Earl's Court Hippies** are usually considered to be 'prehistoric' – the missing link between Alex Korner and the first, mist-shrouded skifflers to scuttle about near the entrance to Charing X tube station. (Circa 1952, possibly the Dements or the Toms. Ed.)

KODAK SAFETY FILM
KODAK SAFETY FILM
KODAK SAFETY FILM

"Tubular Bells
happened very
quickly. It was
a phenomenal
success. Founded
the company
really."
Ken Berry

"Mike was very retiring, an incredible talent, and if he could have been as outward-going when he was a teenager as he is today, if he'd actually toured at the time (which we desperately tried to persuade him to do), he could have continued to be as big as any band before or since. I mean another of his records, *Omnadawn* is so beautiful and for me the best record he's ever made, but in Mike's case, perhaps because of his refusal to tour, *Tubular Bells* became more famous than he did. The one and only concert I'd managed to arrange with him to perform was at the Queen Elizabeth Hall. We'd been to see a host of quite celebrated musicians, played each of them *Tubular Bells*, and persuaded them to come for this one-off gig. Every seat in the house was completely sold out when at the Manor, the day before the show, Mike said that he couldn't go through with it; he just couldn't do it. Whether through a flash of instinct, desperation, I don't know what it was, but I owned a beautiful old Bentley at the time which I'd bought from George Harrison and which I knew he wanted. So I simply said, 'Look Mike, if you do the show, you can have my car. Here are the keys, you get them tomorrow night.' The psychological block somehow got sorted out, because he suddenly looked up and said, 'O.K. - I'll do it!' And as it turned out, the concert was a truly magnificent success! I mean, I remember tears coming down - it was just one of those absolutely wonderful nights."

R. B.

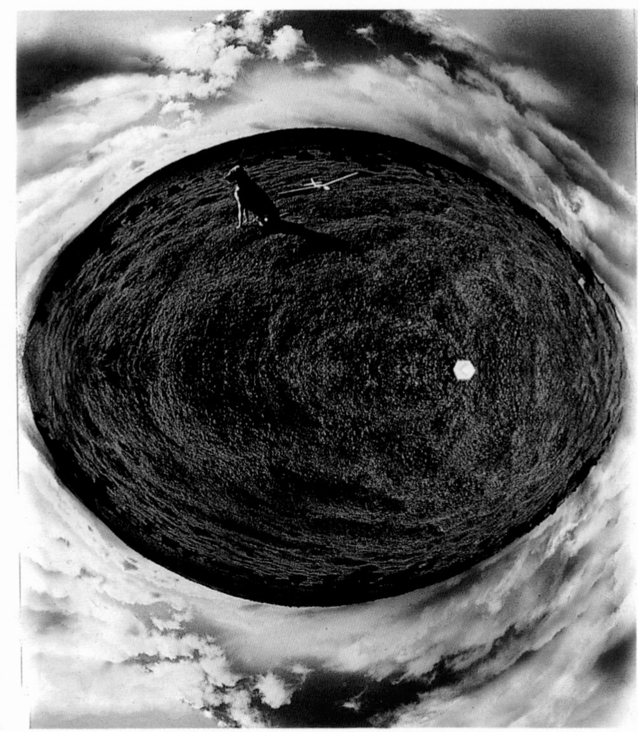

"I first met Mike when he was playing bass for Kevin Ayers and the Whole World. Then, when he was doing some session work at the Manor he played Tom Newman and Simon Hayworth, who were running the recording studio, this tape of his music. They were impressed, to put it mildly, played the tape to me and it was just staggeringly good. It was really incredible because it was the whole first twenty minutes of *Tubular Bells*, pretty much as it appeared on the record. Over-dubbing was very much in its infancy then, but by putting little bits of card over the recording heads of this tiny four track-tape recorder, he'd somehow managed to create a record at his home, this wonderful, intricate piece of music. So when we began the record label a few months later, he was the first person I called up, and after we'd actually signed him, he worked at the Manor re-recording what he'd done so far, and then he just carried right on, creating and finishing the rest of the piece. As soon as people heard it, they were bowled over - right from the day I introduced it to the Island Records sales force, who along with EMI, were distributing our records for us. It just took off and gathered momentum in a massive way because it was so extraordinary, so different from anything else."

S. D.

'Gong' was one of the first of the out-of-the-mainstream (and well-into-the-woods in my view, Ed.) groups to be signed by Dick Branson's fledgling Virgin Records. Pictured here in one of their seasonal outings, they were

a multi-national group with a flexible lineup, most frequently led by David Allen (vocals and guitar), providing an effervescent mix of avant-garde and jazz rock, with hypnotic chants and eerie 'space-whisper' vocals.

"I never heard it directly from anyone, but I was told that EMI, who were our co-distributors in the U.K. with Island, called us the Earl's Court Hippies. They weren't quite sure what we were, but they knew we all had long hair and for some reason thought we were in Earl's Court."

K. B.

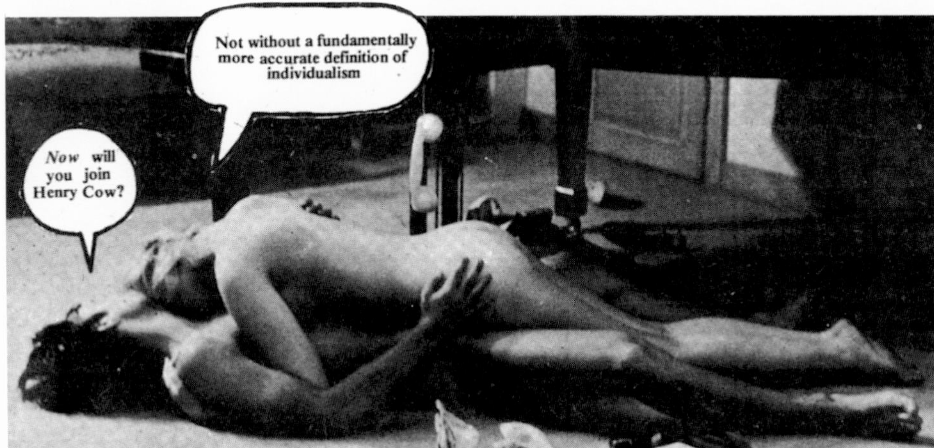

gong

"It's quite a mixture of characters and personalities and really was like Simon building his own record collection, a kind of personal obsession–which actually I think can be a good reason for doing anything."

RICHARD BRANSON

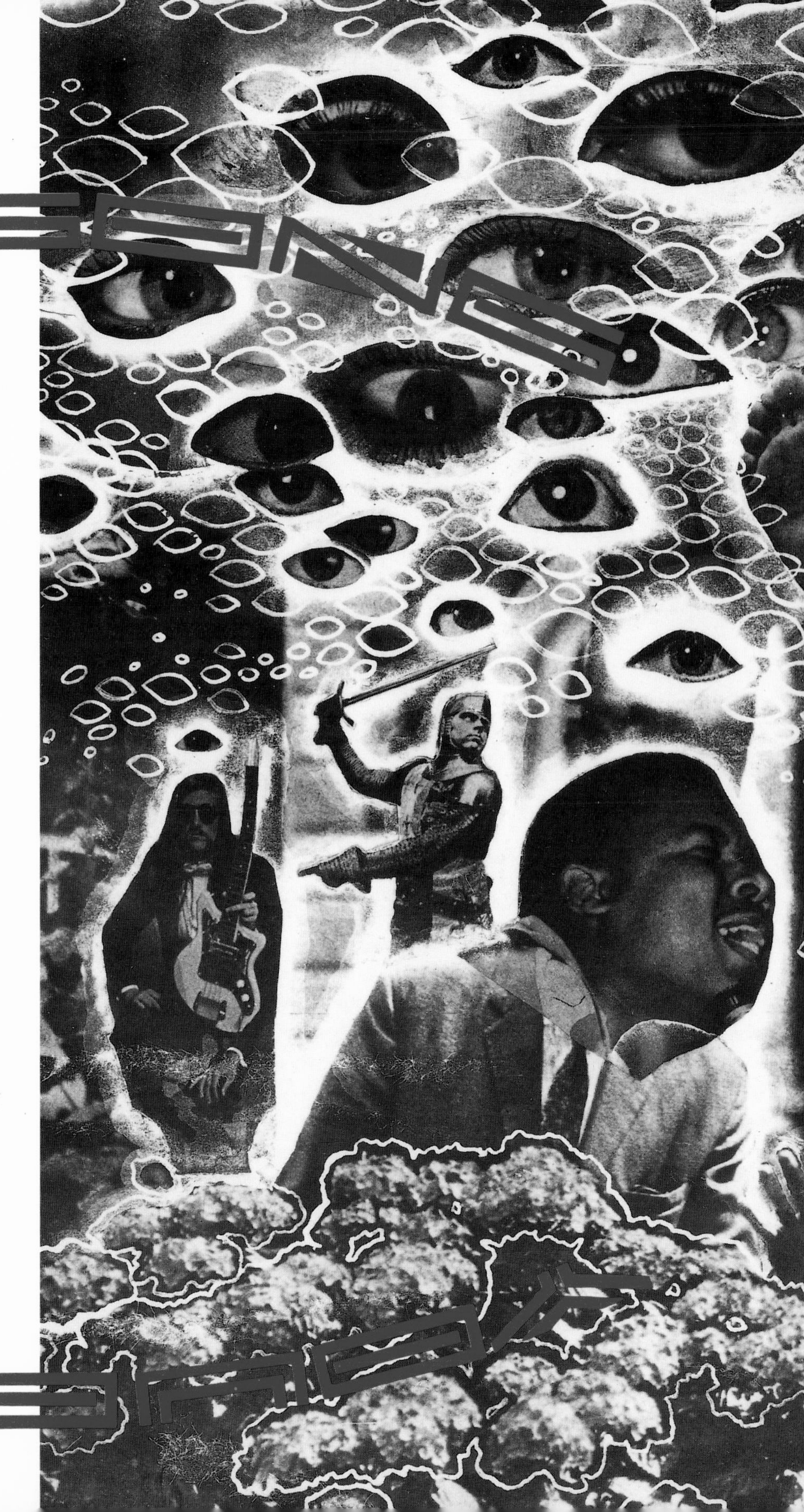

Artwork by 'Lady June' for 'Lady June's Linguistic Leprosy'

3. *Hatfield And The North.* A great new British band, and one of the latest releases from the excellent Virgin label. If I were a musician, then this would be my ideal album. Snorting saxes, tinkling pianos, rippling guitar chords, neat drum patterns and just listen to the bass! Who could ask for more? It would be a great pity if this band didn't make it, as they have as much talent as any band you care to mention.

Let it Rock - May 1974

A roadside respite to break their long journey northwards, the curious Hatfield celebrate their early Virgin signing by decanting a few bottles of bubbly and "letting their minds roll on." (We shall hear more of their stay later. Ed.)

Hatfield and the North

No stranger to the cozy **hearth** an traditional family **values**, accordionist Mr. **Les Nicholson**, if indeed that is his name, is thought by many to be a "dead ringer" for the American thesp. **Don Sutherland** in certain half lights – no offense, Don. "**None taken**," said the good-natured mummer when queried for a response.

slapp happy

"**Lady June** threw a party in her mansion flat at Maida Vale, during the course of which Robert Wyatt took a very **pretty young woman** into the bathroom. After a little while his wife started banging on the door, so to escape the situation, Robert tried to climb out of the window onto the drainpipe, but tragically **he slipped**, fell two floors, and ended up permanently confined to a wheelchair. It was awful for everyone involved and completely devastating of course for Robert. But a few months later he and his wife came up with this idea for a poster—**she'd got him back!**"

S.D.

lady june

CAPTAIN BEEFHEART LOOKS AT LIFE

(or, The Saga of Captain Beefy)

His Talent
I am a genius and there's nothing I can do about it.

LSD
An awfully overrated aspirin and very similar to old peoples' Disneyland.

Shakespeare
He was out licking the sidewalks to feel the texture of the souls. I've licked a few sidewalks myself.

Race
Everybody's coloured or else you wouldn't be able to see them.

The Consumer Society
A carrot is as close as a rabbit gets to a diamond.

Drugs
It's not worth getting into the bullshit to see what the bull ate.

Evolution
I think that man has the most highly developed intelligence. I think men get so intelligent that they're stupid.

Virgin Records
They're so old-fashioned. I've seen better jokes in bubble-gum wrappers.

Mike Oldfield
Corn, pure corn. Comparing that young sprout to Stravinsky, *Tubular Bells* or whatever the name is. That's disgusting. I left the table.

Mental Health
The largest flying land mammal is the absent mind.

"Revolutionary Cinema"
Oh, that's wonderful. You mean before, their cameras weren't turning?

"Captain Beefheart was a great guy. I remember walking down the street with him in Los Angeles when his wife had to walk five yards behind him, and occasionally he'd turn around to declare, 'Take that down!' He didn't actually have to say that at all, however, because her full-time job appeared to be to promptly scribble down, for posterity, each word he uttered – all of his wonderful discourses on everything and everyone."

R.B.

"Working in Nashville felt like what I'd been looking for all those years. Those session musicians were shit-hot, and I was having to sing like a bitch to keep up, but we were in a log cabin with a field of cows out the front, corn on the cob growing in the backyard, and there was no bullshit – just people making music."

CAROL GRIMES

Trumpet player extraordinaire Lol Coxhill treated the audience to some particularly inspired lunacy interlaced with fine music.

M.M. 17.10.73

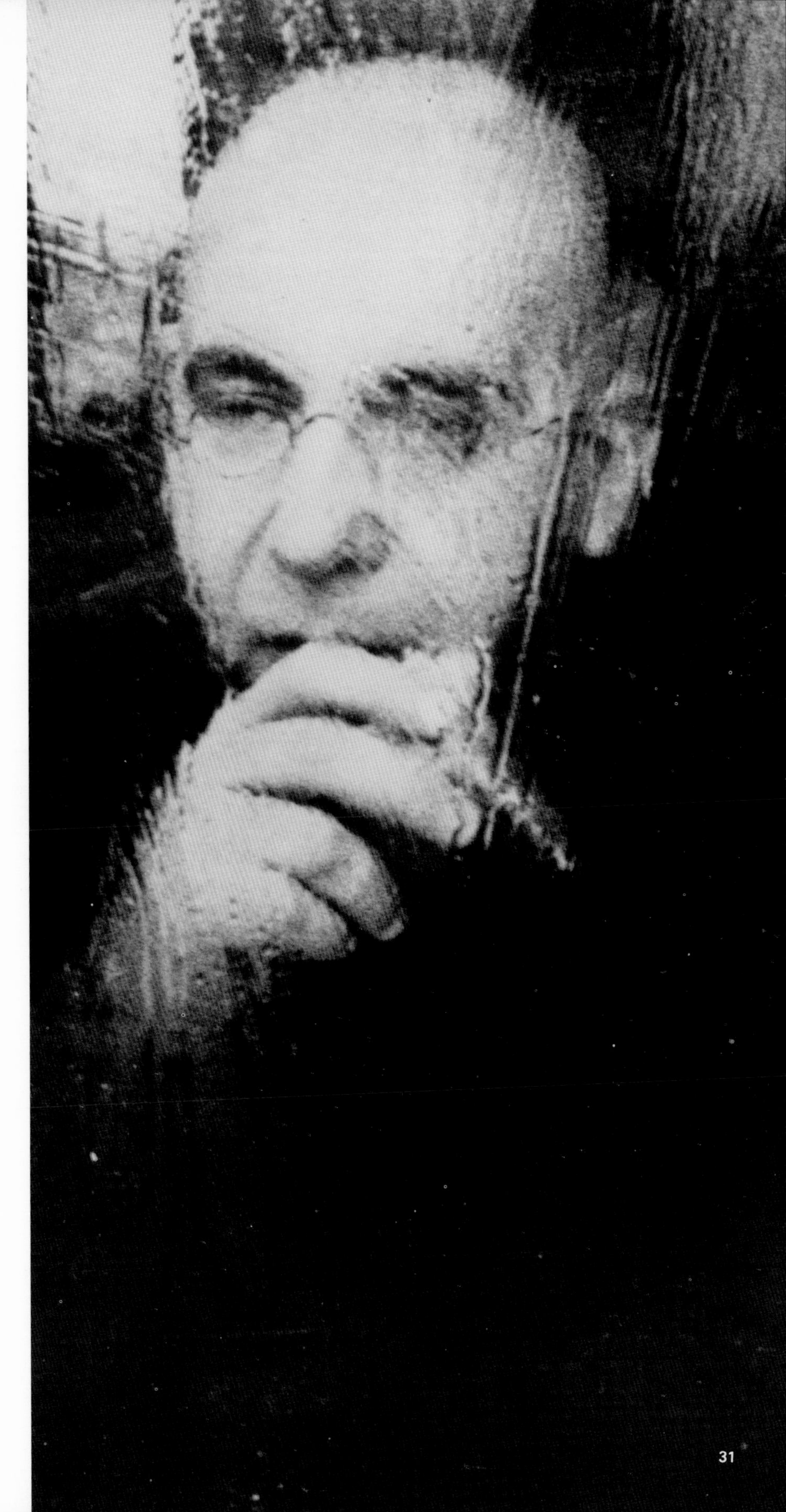

Press Release :

STONES PLEAD WITH VIRGIN SENSATION ......

In spite of pleas from the Rolling Stones, Virgin Records will go ahead with their Henry Cow/Kevin Coyne concert at the Commonwealth Institute on Kensington High Street at 7.30 p.m. Saturday 8th September. Kevin Coyne and Henry Cow will perform songs from their new album released this week on the Virgin label. It is felt the Stones are mortally afraid that the Coyne/Henry Cow gig, coinciding as it does with their Wembley Stadium appearance will seriously jeopardise their future.

"The Commonwealth Institute seats only 429" a Virgin Spokesman added "but the individual seats are very large". We are expecting a monster.........

'Burning guitars means nothing'

"This whole thing of bloody burning guitars," explodes the volatile Moore, "and all that crap. It means nothing. Absolutely NOTHING!"

PETER BAUMANN: "Without Debussy, Presley, Beatles, Pink Floyd, Tangerine Dream would be impossible."

Tangerine Dream Victoria Palace

THE AUDIENCE at any of their concerts can in no way expect to be entertained," warned the programme notes for Tangerine Dream's British debut.

EVENING STANDARD 8.10.'73

"Tom Newman co-produced *Tubular Bells* – he's a great guy who I'm sure helped Mike a great deal. I wouldn't be at all surprised if some of the humor, like the Vivian Stanshall bits, didn't come from Tom."
R.B.

"Since the acceptance of bacteria as a life form, bacteria bridge clubs have sprung up all over. . . A whole tournament can be over in one tenth of a second; you should see them deal."
IVOR CUTLER, VELVET DONKEY '75

"Pictured here on the left in conference with John Varnom, Al Clark became our press officer in '74. Instead of spending fortunes taking out advertising, we would 'target' certain people. Al used to take journalists on foreign trips, with different bands, and he used to get, for a relatively small amount of money, the airfares, etc., monster coverage – three-page features in N.M.E. and M.M., for instance. There always seemed to be a tremendous amount of drinking and womanizing with Al and this great assortment of truly funny artistes – and in those days the music papers were incredibly influential. N.M.E., for example, used to have a circulation of 400,000." S.D.

john varnom

Mr. **Simon Draper** has yet to explain how he came across this shack and his discovery inside of **Link Wray**, an authentic white-trash dirtfarm exponent, indeed master, of the H. Ledbetter persuasion.

WRAY
SHACK

LINK
WRAY
STUCK IN GEAR

THE GREAT DUDU PUKWANA LIMBERS HIS AXE BEFORE THE GIG

... and gives the old gourd a breather between sets.

Kevin Ayers was Bryan Ferry before Bryan Ferry. He had a great voice, women adored him and he was always going to happen. He'd put out a record, the vibe would be great, but then he'd fuck off for six months: "Oh man, I must go off and do some scuba-diving". Consequently he kept blowing it. Don't believe you never get a second chance, he had lots of chances, he had enormous talent, but he could never get his brain around developing his career. He just thought there were more important things in life than being a pop star. At least he never let the pop music get to him, he never thought it was that important. It was just an excuse to get someone to pick up the bills for the champagne and the scuba-diving!

Q Magazine '89

"Kevin Ayers is important to Virgin even though, irony of ironies, we only put out one album with him, quite later on, when he was definitely not on his top form. But he was a friend and a constant influence and presence throughout, really. I mean, I only knew about and came to sign Mike Oldfield, for example, because he played in Kevin Ayers' band."

S.D.

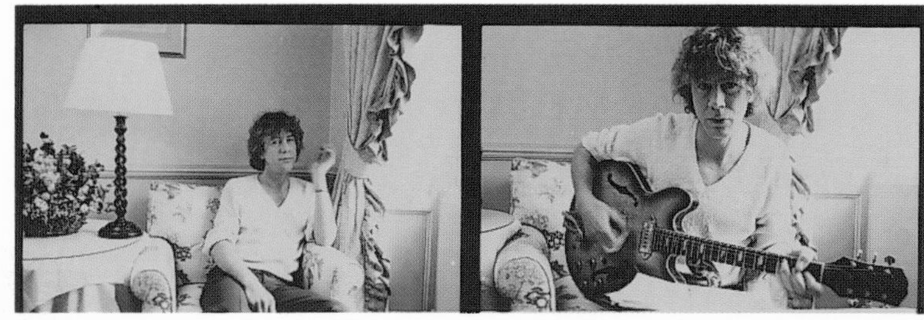

kevin ayers

"One of Virgin's mistakes over th years, I think, was not droppin bands. We always were very prou that we stuck with people for year and years and sometimes it worked with Simple Minds, for example. Bu David we did drop as an artiste so he wrote me a charming lette saying how much he understoo the fact that we'd had to dro him, and he wrote a letter t Mike saying what complete an utter bastards we were, an he put each letter in th wrong envelope!"

R.B

"If I made as much noise with my music as the neighbours' dogs do then I'd get complaints from all over the place. But barking seems an accepted part of life."

“We’re the first band Virgin have signed who don’t wear woolly hats . . .

“This one, Albie Donelly, used to be so funny. He’d come down from Liverpool and say, ‘I’m just going down to see how my album’s coming on.’ Then he’d pop into the studio and just have a listen for an hour or so, because Matt Wanger did just about everything on the records – played all the instruments, sang all the parts, wrote all the songs! In spite of Matt’s involvement, all of Supercharge could play. They were great live! Fantastic! And we put a lot of effort into them, but they never had a hit.”
S.D.

Albie ponders the possibility of a Jeannie Bobbit in his future.

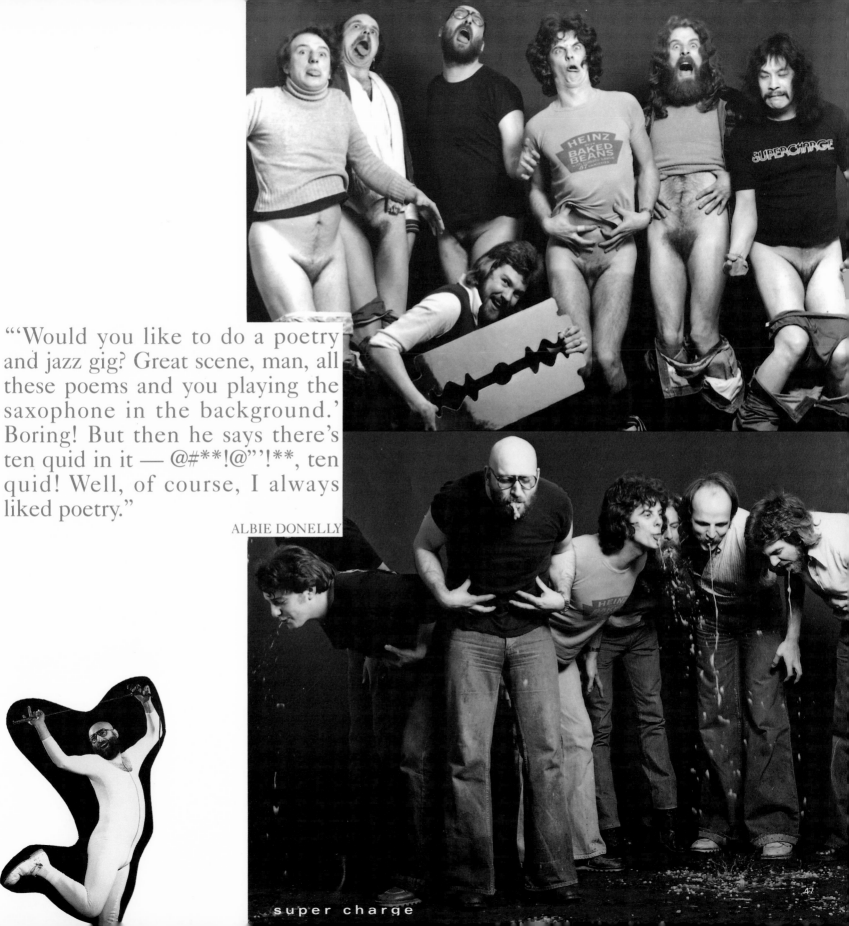

“‘Would you like to do a poetry and jazz gig? Great scene, man, all these poems and you playing the saxophone in the background.’ Boring! But then he says there’s ten quid in it — @#**!@”’!**, ten quid! Well, of course, I always liked poetry.”

ALBIE DONELLY

super charge

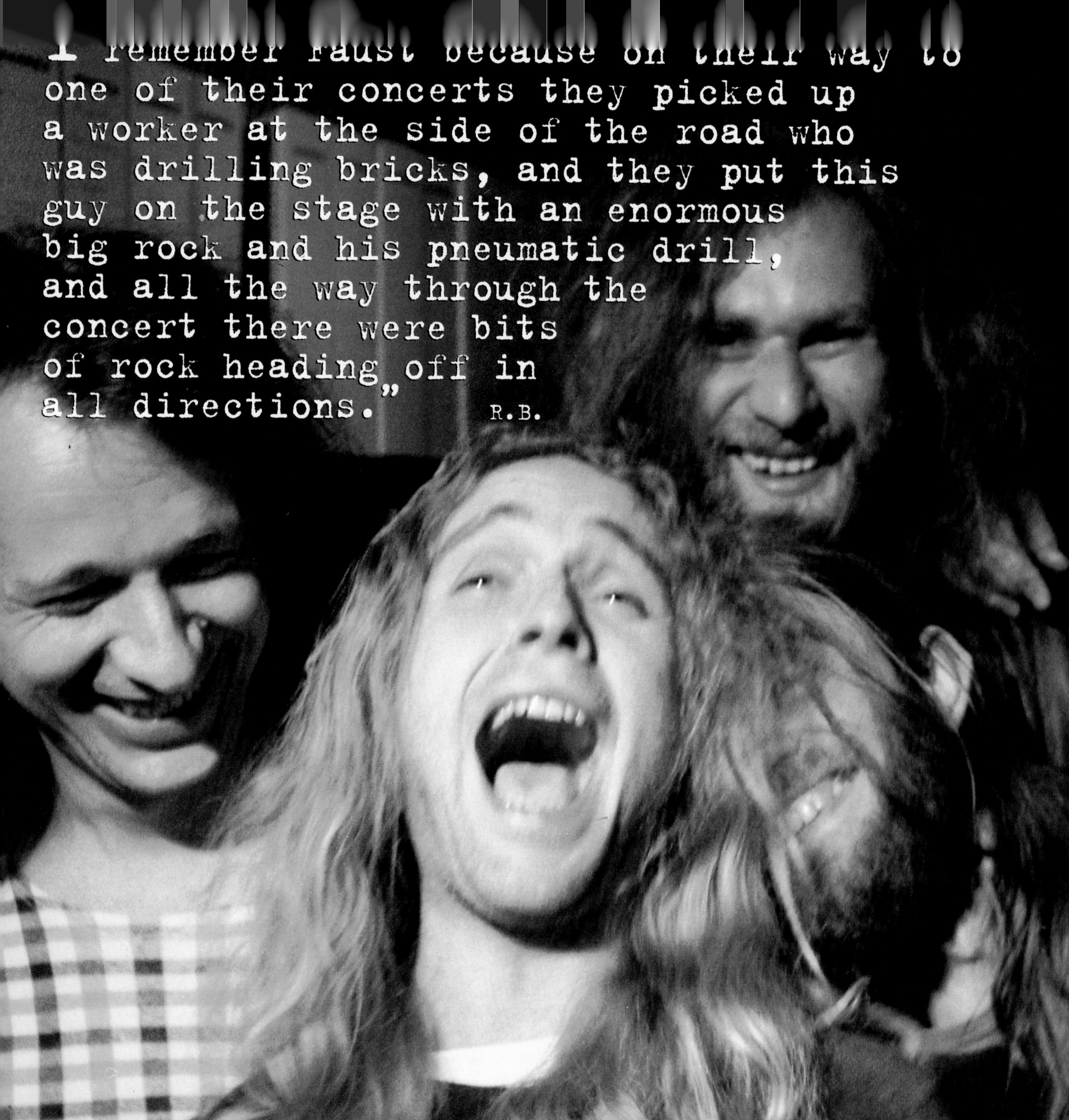
I remember Faust because on their way to
one of their concerts they picked up
a worker at the side of the road who
was drilling bricks, and they put this
guy on the stage with an enormous
big rock and his pneumatic drill,
and all the way through the
concert there were bits
of rock heading off in
all directions."
R.B.

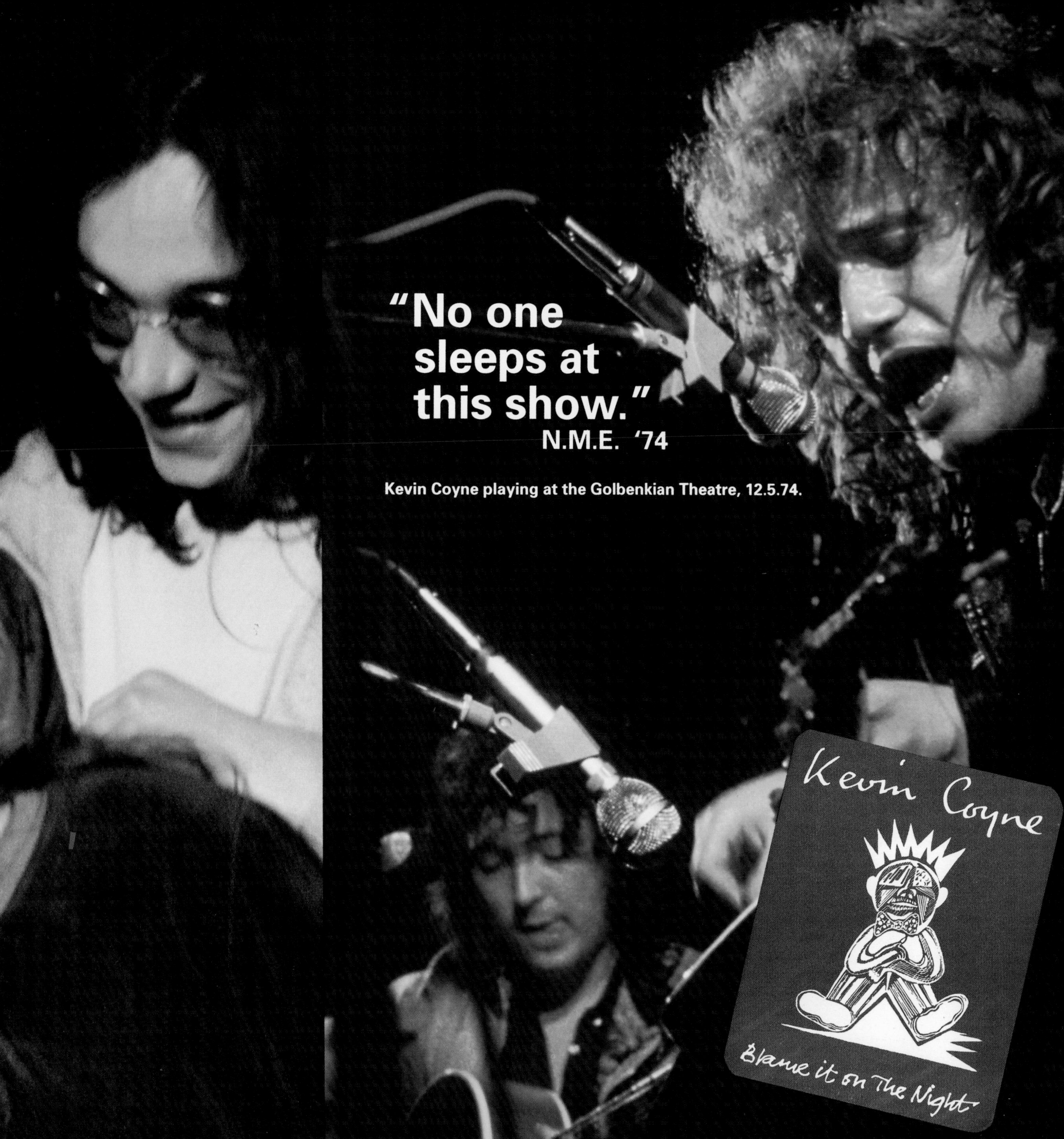

Kevin Coyne playing at the Golbenkian Theatre, 12.5.74.

"I had a dog called Yellow Dog in Portugal, and he really was bright yellow. I couldn't bring him back into Britain because of quarantine laws. Our cat's over there as well. He's famous – he's appeared on the radio!"

HERBIE ARMSTRONG

richard branson

In one of the most astonishing, and unfortunate, co-incidences in the annals of recorded time, the long-awaited and pricelessly historic **Silver Jubilee in England,** occurred at the same time as the album debut of an upstart – indeed, anarchistic – group called

the Sex Pistols.

In an appalling affront to the Crown, the Royal Household, and the beloved HMQ herself, the album, issued without apology by Dick Branson's Virgin Records, featured a salacious rendition of "God Save the Queen," as well as artwork on the album cover depicting **the Queen** as a kind of harridan with her most favourable features blacked out by what appeared to be the trappings of bondage. Apparently not satisfied with having tainted and spoiled her cherished Jubilee, the culprits (for so they were generally regarded) proceeded to deface the fabled monuments of the city of London, as well as the popular double-decker bus, with garish posters proclaiming "God Save..." and substituting for "the Queen" the names of a nightmarish array of rogues and scoundrels of the most infamous nature: the ruthless highwayman, feisty **Dick Turpin,** the spunky cutthroat pirate, Captain Swing, Jack the Ripper, etc., etc., ad nauseam.

The success of the album so infuriated the general public that the music industry apparently had no qualms about actually arranging to keep the record off what some would term the "charmed" or "lucky" Number One spot.

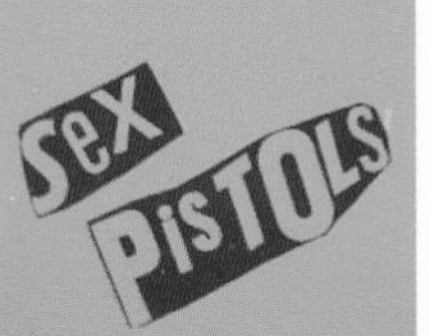

"One day I heard this music coming through the floor from down below, and it was 'Anarchy in the U.K.' I remember running all the way downstairs and saying to Simon, 'What's that? – it sounds fantastic,' and Simon saying, 'It's the Sex Pistols, they've just signed to EMI.' I then went back to my office, rang up EMI, and in those days they wouldn't actually take a call, the chairman wouldn't talk to me direct, but he decided I could talk to his secretary, so I left a message saying that if he wants to get rid of his embarrassment, can he give me a ring. I got a curt message back saying, 'We're not embarrassed at all, very happy with the Sex Pistols. Thank you very much.' That same night, the Sex Pistols went on the Bill Grundy show, swearing left, right, and centre, and the next morning, at six a.m. I was woken up at my home by the chairman himself. He asked if I could come over right away. When I arrived, he said, 'Here's the contract! If you want them, you can have them!'

"So then there was the court case over the word *bollocks* – with John Mortimer defending, and he said, 'Well, look – try to find a linguistics expert if you can, who can talk about *bollocks*.' So I rang Nottingham University and asked to speak with the professor of linguistics, and the professor said, 'You mean they're prosecuting you for the word *bollocks*?' I said, 'Well, yes.' He said, 'That's absolute cobblers. The word *bollocks* is not derived from testicles; it's a nickname that was given to the priests of the eighteenth century. Would you like me to come along to the court and tell them that?' I said, 'I'd be delighted.' He then said, 'I happen to be a priest myself, would you like me to wear my dog collar?' So we won that case!"

R.B.

COLD
SOBER
HELLO
ITS
STONE
COLD
SOBER
AGAIN

"I don't give a fuck for any of them – I mean, I never even liked the Stones. Jagger was always too distant. No way could you ever imagine talking to 'Michael Jagger' like you could talk to someone on the street. And you should be able to. I don't see why he has to have fucking bodyguards carting him about all over the place."

JOHN LYDON

"He came down to Sex (McLaren's shop in the King's Road) one afternoon – stood outside for three hours 'cos he was terrified to come inside."

SID VICIOUS

"We was just in it for the piss-up and the birds after the show . . ."

STEVE JONES

SEX PISTOLS

TOP 20 POPS
1 FIRST CUT IS THE DEEPEST ROD STEWART
2
3 LUCILLE KENNY ROGERS
4 EVERGREEN BARBRA STREISAND
5 AIN'T GONNA BUMP NO MORE JOE TEX
6 SHOW YOU THE WAY TO GO JACKSONS
7 YOU'RE MOVING OUT TODAY CAROLE BAYER SAGER
8 THE SHUFFLE VAN MCCOY
9 GOOD MORNING JUDGE 10CC
10 HALF WAY DOWN THE STAIRS MUPPETS
11 GOT TO GIVE IT UP MARVIN GAYE
12 O.K. ROCK FOLLIES
13 TELEPHONE LINE E.L.O.
14 LIDO SHUFFLE BOZ SCAGGS
15 TOKYO JOE BRIAN FERRY
16 DISCO INFERNO TRAMMPS
17 TOO HOT TO HANDLE HEATWAVE
18 GONNA CAPTURE YOUR HEART BLUE
19 WE CAN DO IT LIVERPOOL TEAM
20 MAH NA MAH NA PIERO UMILIANI

"We wouldn't have dreamt of accusing anyone of fiddling with the charts, but the fact that all our research showed that 'God Save the Queen' was easily out-selling any other record in the U.K., and the fact that it was only listed in the charts as a blank, did make us wonder whether there wasn't some motivation to achieve a result other than its becoming Number One during the Silver Jubilee Week." **K.B.**

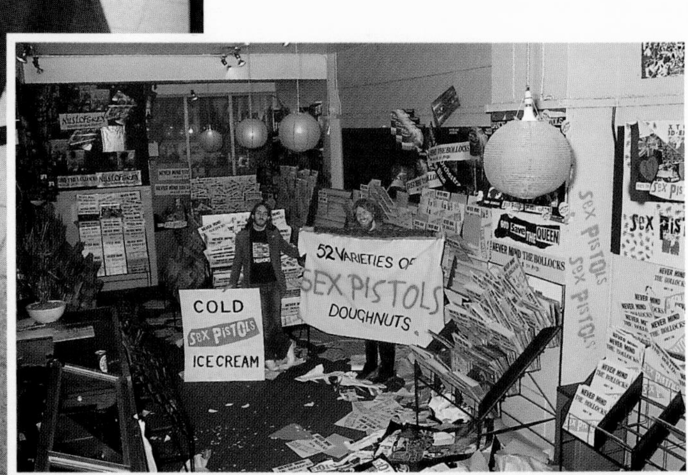

“They can shut us out but never shut us up.”

JOHN LYDON

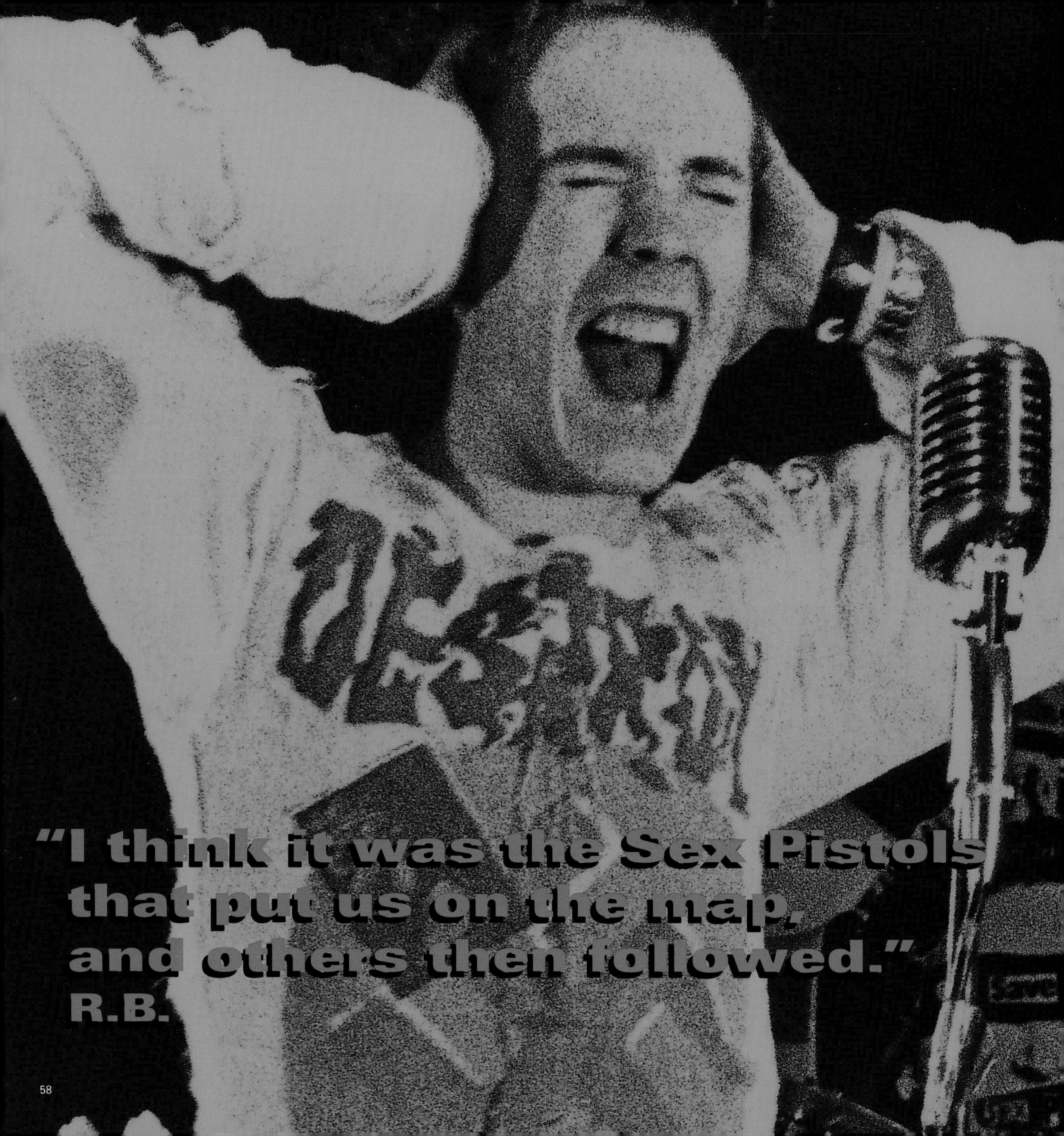

"I think it was the Sex Pistols that put us on the map, and others then followed."
R.B.

sid vicious and his mum

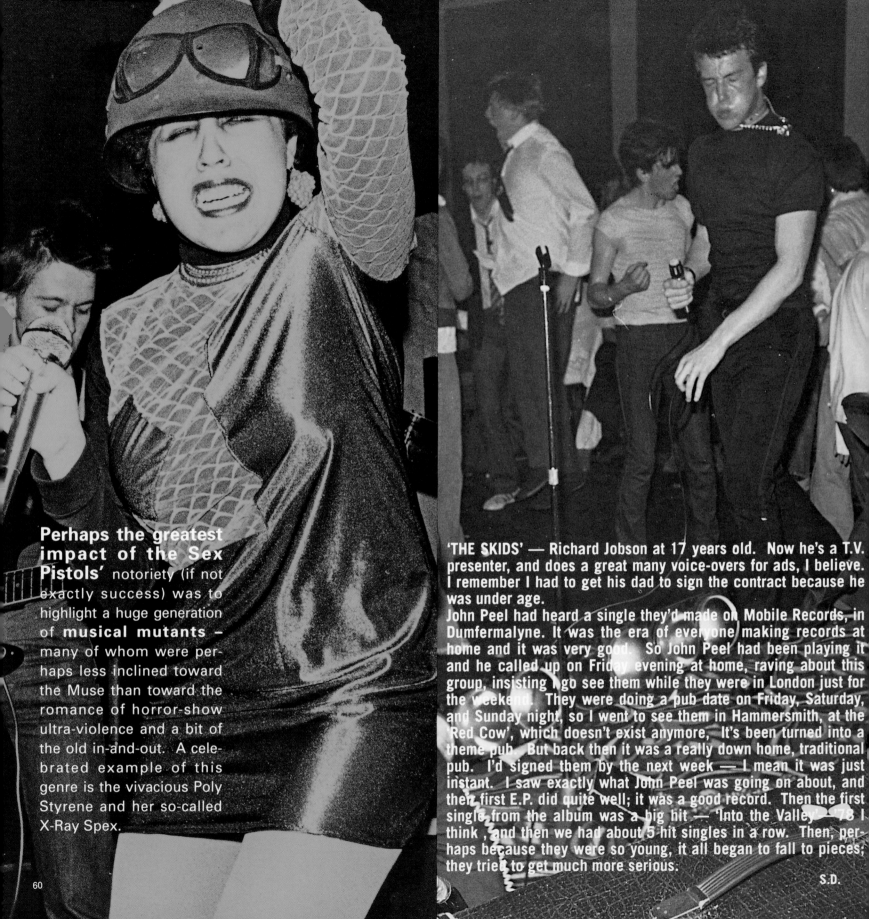

Perhaps the greatest impact of the Sex Pistols' notoriety (if not exactly success) was to highlight a huge generation of **musical mutants** – many of whom were perhaps less inclined toward the Muse than toward the romance of horror-show ultra-violence and a bit of the old in-and-out. A celebrated example of this genre is the vivacious Poly Styrene and her so-called X-Ray Spex.

'THE SKIDS' — Richard Jobson at 17 years old. Now he's a T.V. presenter, and does a great many voice-overs for ads, I believe. I remember I had to get his dad to sign the contract because he was under age.

John Peel had heard a single they'd made on Mobile Records, in Dumfermalyne. It was the era of everyone making records at home and it was very good. So John Peel had been playing it and he called up on Friday evening at home, raving about this group, insisting I go see them while they were in London just for the weekend. They were doing a pub date on Friday, Saturday, and Sunday night, so I went to see them in Hammersmith, at the 'Red Cow', which doesn't exist anymore, It's been turned into a theme pub. But back then it was a really down home, traditional pub. I'd signed them by the next week — I mean it was just instant. I saw exactly what John Peel was going on about, and their first E.P. did quite well; it was a good record. Then the first single from the album was a big hit — 'Into the Valley' — '78 I think , and then we had about 5 hit singles in a row. Then, perhaps because they were so young, it all began to fall to pieces; they tried to get much more serious.

S.D.

'The Skids', no sticklers for formality, inexorably cutting a rug toward a dark and certain tryst... if only with the boys in blue.

"We love rock'n'roll and want to enjoy ourselves. We're absolutely committed to Penetration and rock'n'roll. Rock'n'roll through Penetration. It's very awe—inspiring you know that if it's a duff gig it's you you're letting down, no-one else."

Vying with the fab Poly S for center stage is XTC of dazzling *White Music* fame giving no quarter and asking none.

● "We play notes that other people won't have anything to do with. We befriend these drunken tramp notes that hide in the dirty corners of your instrument." — Andy Partridge, XTC,

"I used to look at groups and things and think, I want to do it. I'd have daydreams of me being onstage doing it and enjoying it. And I did it and I haven't any real talent, except I blag well."

NICKY TESCO

"The Ruts – Malcolm Owen – they were great and would've been a huge band if he hadn't self-destructed on heroin." S.D.

"I did so much speed I used to rattle, but I can't take the buzz anymore. And smack just makes you selfish."

–Malcolm Owen

the members

THE MOTORS, having been completely cleared of charges by the Crown of "heinous conduct with S/M apparati," are now able to resume their study of "new routines."

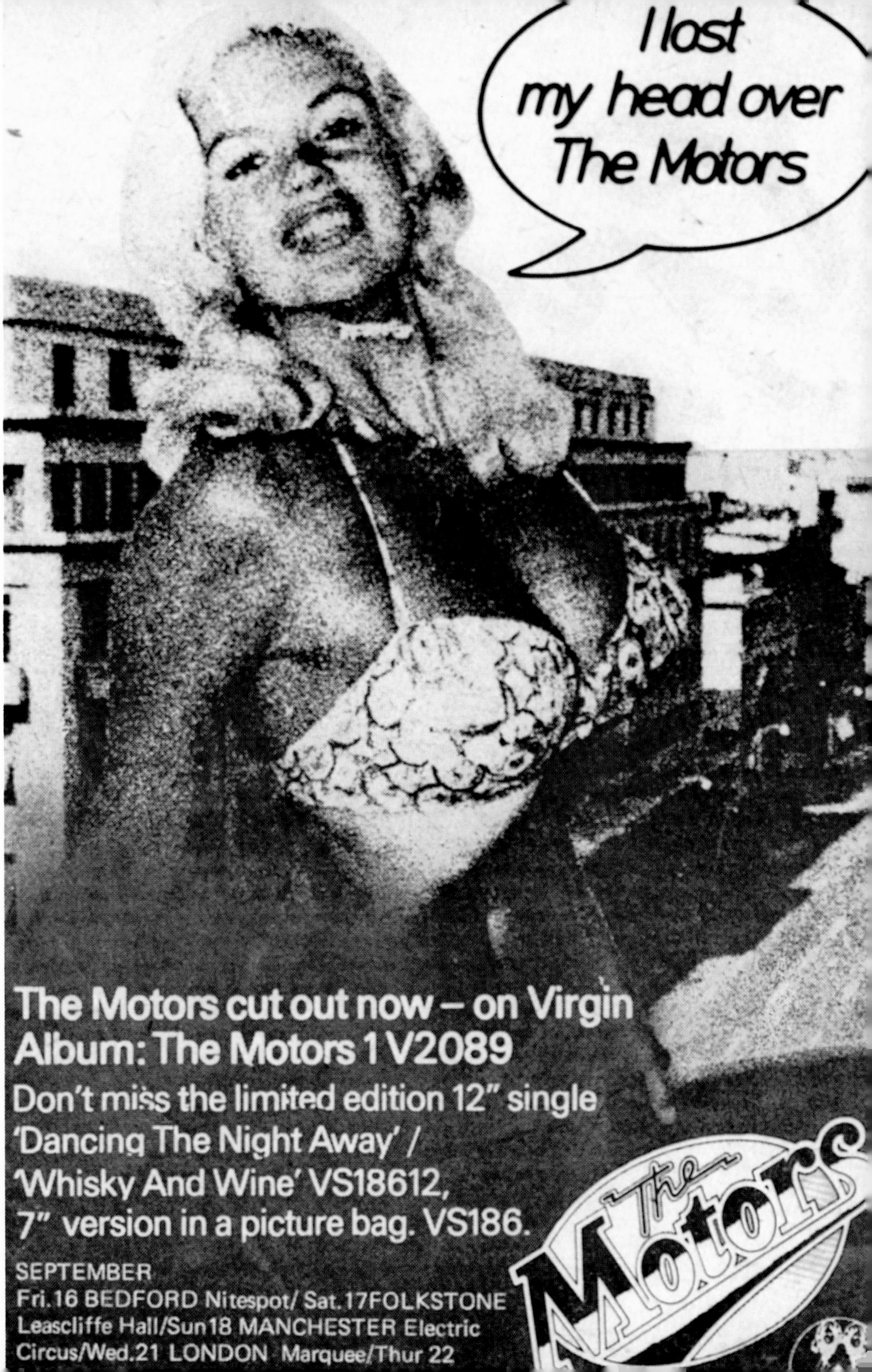

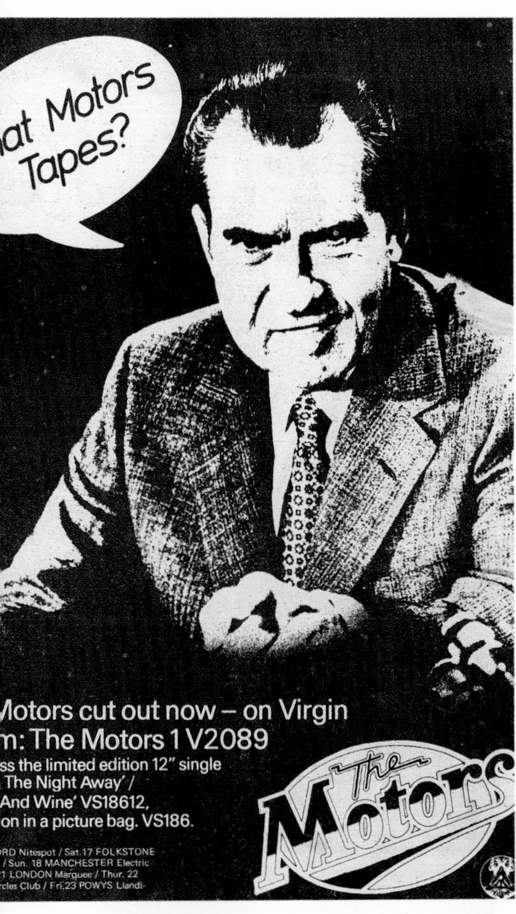

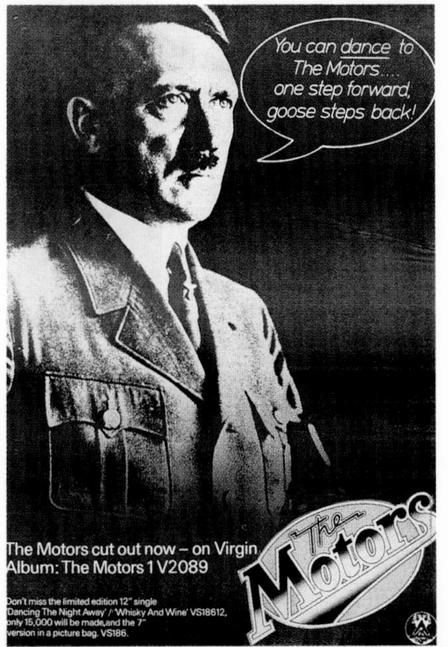

I lost my head over The Motors
The Motors cut out now – on Virgin
Album: The Motors 1 V2089
Don't miss the limited edition 12" single
'Dancing The Night Away' /
'Whisky And Wine' VS18612,
7" version in a picture bag. VS186.
The Motors
SEPTEMBER
Fri.16 BEDFORD Nitespot/ Sat.17FOLKSTONE
Leascliffe Hall/Sun18 MANCHESTER Electric
Circus/Wed.21 LONDON Marquee/Thur 22

at Motors Tapes?
Aotors cut out now – on Virgin
n: The Motors 1 V2089
ss the limited edition 12" single
The Night Away' /
And Wine' VS18612,
ion in a picture bag. VS186.
The Motors
RD Nitespot / Sat.17 FOLKSTONE
/ Sun. 18 MANCHESTER Electric
21 LONDON Marquee / Thur. 22
rcles Club / Fri.23 POWYS Llandi-

You can dance to The Motors… one step forward, goose steps back!
The Motors cut out now – on Virgin
Album: The Motors 1 V2089
Don't miss the limited edition 12" single
'Dancing The Night Away' / 'Whisky And Wine' VS18612,
only 15,000 will be made, and the 7"
version in a picture bag. VS186.
The Motors

One of Cook/Moore's more extravagant, and ambitious, productions was of course a fifteen-minute audio epic called "Exploring Joan Crawford's Cavernous Vagina." The basic conceit of the piece was that these two young English speciologists had accidentally come upon this mysterious cave in the Hollywood Hills. They cautiously enter; when their eyes become accustomed to the darkness, they are astonished by the immensity of it. "It is fucking monumental!" exclaims Moore. "Hmmm," Cook agrees, "a bit scary, isn't it? What's that peculiar smell?"

They begin their explorations, tentatively at first, then growing bolder, discovering one odd thing after another – a gully here, a small gurgling thermal pool there, two cashmere sweaters, three bracelets, half a dozen earrings, two pair of women's high-heel shoes. "There is something vaguely familiar about all this," says Cook. "Yes, hauntingly so," Moore agrees, "but I just can't seem to get a proper purchase on it." "Quite," says Cook. "What the hell is this place?" What finally tips them off as to the true nature of their environs is the discovery of a lilac-scented diary. "Is this the smell you were talking about?" Cook wants to know as he puts it under Moore's nose. "No , no, that's bloody lilac," says Moore. "The smell I'm talking about – I can still smell it, you know – is more like – more antiseptic, do you know what I'm saying?" "Well, I do know the smell of antiseptics, for God's sake, Dudley. Do you mean like Listerine, that sort of thing, Lysol?" "Yes, Lysol, that's it, that sort of smell. It's gone now." "Uh-huh." Cook's attitude seems changed. "You know where we are now, don't you?" Moore seems surprised. "No, do you?" "You really don't know, do you?" Cook persists. Moore answers in annoyance, "No I don't, Peter," and adds with maniacal calm, "Why don't you tell me?" Cook (fairly shouting): "We are lost in the cunt of Joan Crawford!"

"DEREK AND CLIVE were at the townhouse making this extremely rude record, when suddenly all these police officers came pouring in – dozens of them. So Dudley Moore passed this bit of hash to Peter Cook, who passed it on to Judy Cook and it was going round and round, until eventually, of course, they were all caught and busted. Fortunately for them, however, the officers were actually just people I'd arranged to come storming in dressed up as policemen." R.B.

"JULIE COVINGTON sang 'Don't Cry for Me Argentina' and also sang 'Only Women Bleed.' She'd become a huge star. I mean, it was the biggest-selling record of the year, but a little bit like Mike Oldfield, she just decided that she didn't like being so successful. She refused to appear in the stage production of *Evita* and simply chose not to be a superstar."

R.B.

"I'm not interested in poetry at all. Poetry is – I dunno – *it's smelly.*"

HOWARD DEVOTO

ROTTEN TIME!

Punk star Johnny gets three months for pub punch-up

on bail awaiting appeal

p.i.l.

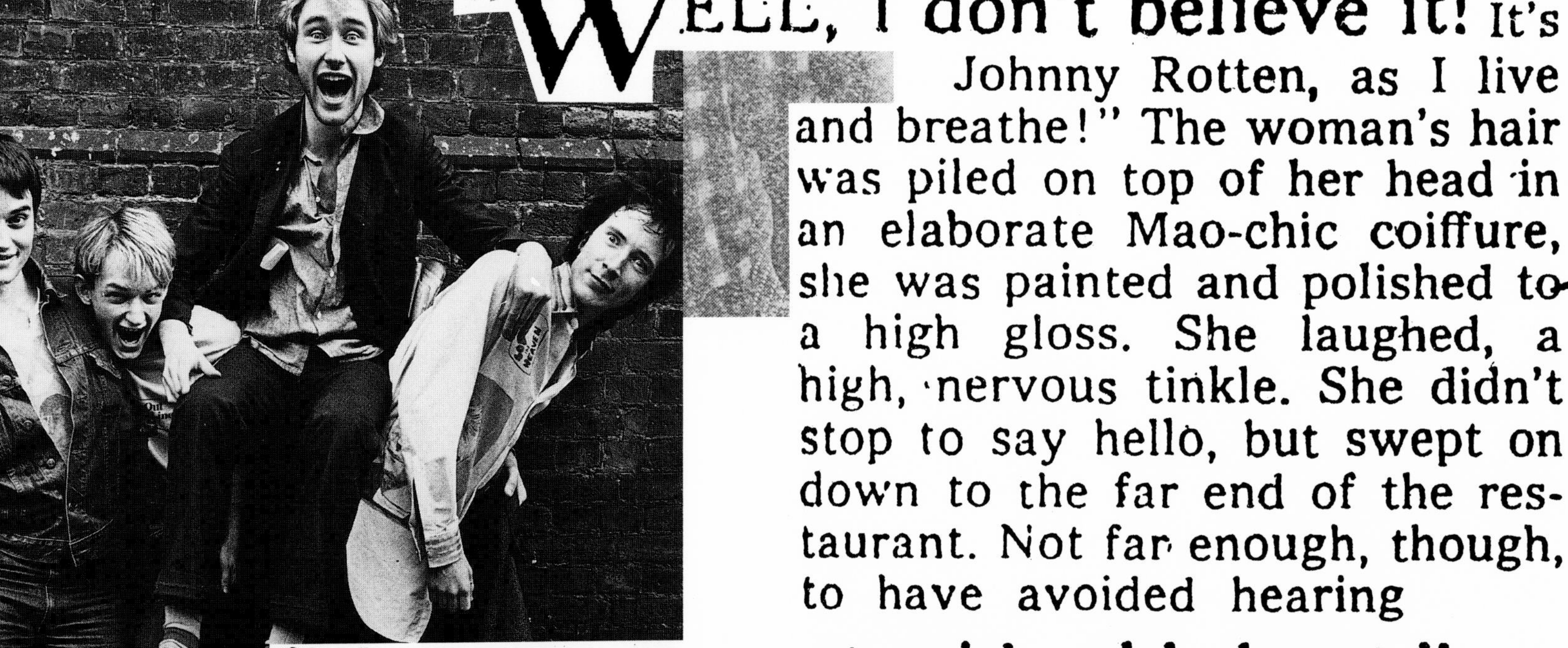

"WELL, I don't believe it! It's Johnny Rotten, as I live and breathe!" The woman's hair was piled on top of her head in an elaborate Mao-chic coiffure, she was painted and polished to a high gloss. She laughed, a high, nervous tinkle. She didn't stop to say hello, but swept on down to the far end of the restaurant. Not far enough, though, to have avoided hearing

"shut up you stupid old boot," and "what are you talking about, you prat," echoing cheerfully behind her from the assembled PIL company.

THE SUN 7.10.80

"What nobody realised was that the Pistols were big business, and far from being manipulated. We were doing the manipulating and winning hands down. I've always wanted to make money; I'm certainly not afraid of wanting it. I'm just not interested in living in a shack, and I'm not interested in failure. We almost certainly earned a lot more than £ 600,000, but that's what's been accounted for so far. Unfortunately, Malcolm McLaren walked off with the whole lot. I've had £ 12,000 up until now, and he owes me at least another £ 60,000. I have views of my own, but I'll never talk about things I don't understand—it's for the middle-class dropouts."

JOHN LYDON

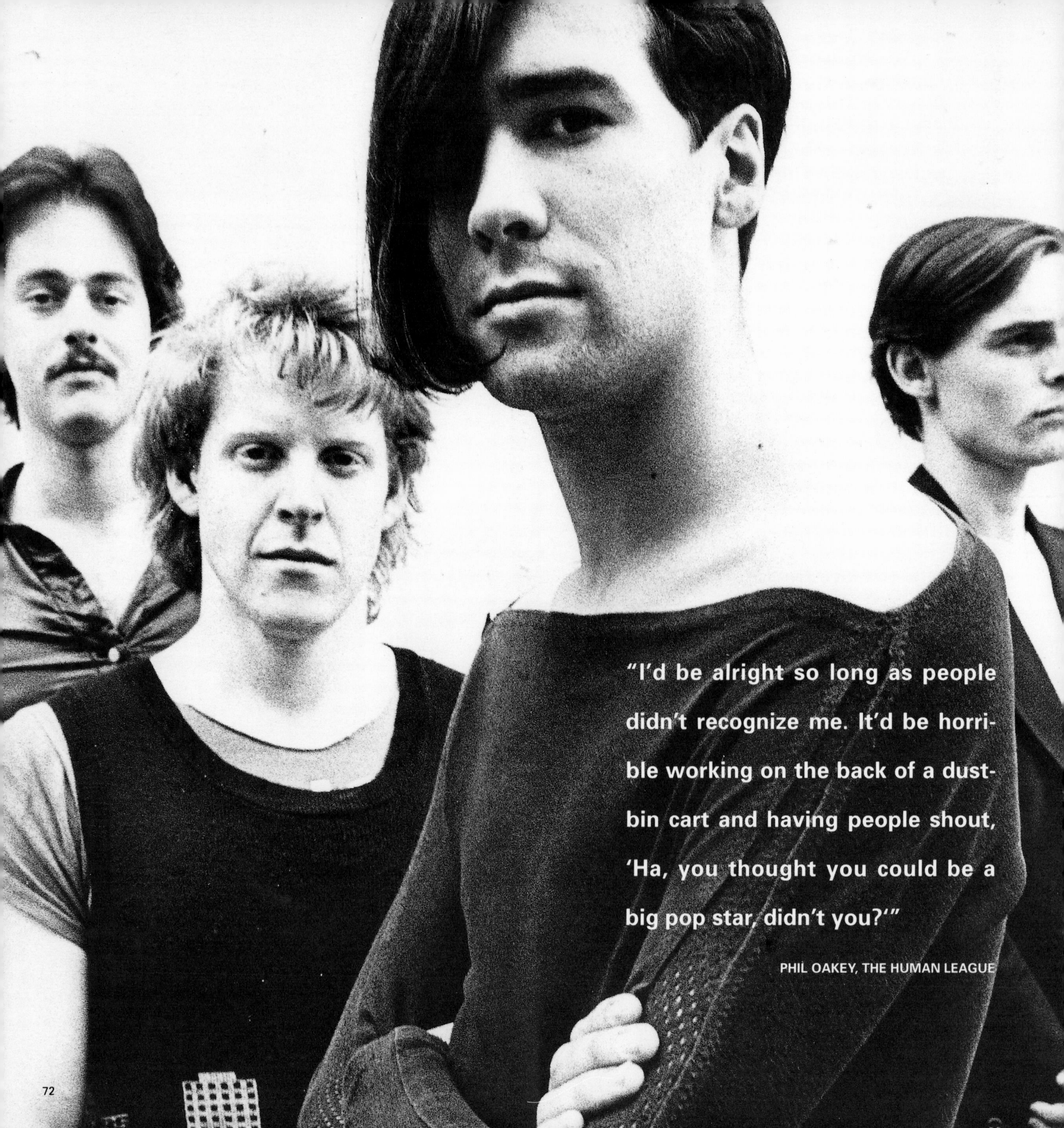

"I'd be alright so long as people didn't recognize me. It'd be horrible working on the back of a dustbin cart and having people shout, 'Ha, you thought you could be a big pop star, didn't you?'"

PHIL OAKEY, THE HUMAN LEAGUE

Can she have **body** and a **voice?**

The answer is yes

This is no con job. The vocals may not be as mind-blowing as the physicals, but Noel is not left to do it alone.

Yorkshire Post '81

The Professionals (sic) go for the early Chippendale effect.

Amazing story in Sid Vicious case

Sid Vicious . . . coma

'SNEAK THIEF KILLED NANCY'

NEW evidence which could clear punk rock star Sid Vicious of his girl friend's murder is being studied by New York police.

It came from a self-confessed drug dealer and police informer called Rockets Redglare.

From IAIN WALKER in New York

He claimed a sneak thief broke into the couple's hotel room while Sid and his girlfriend, Nancy Spungen were in a drug coma.

The thief murdered Nancy with a knife, possibly when she woke and surprised him, Redglare added.

He claimed that he saw a mystery man, identified only as Steve, enter the hotel lobby hours before the murder.

Redglare also claimed that Nancy had a bundle of 100-dollar bills in her purse the morning she died.

But police confirmed there was no money in the room, in the run-down Chelsea Hotel, Manhattan, when the body was found hours later.

Knife

Detectives grew interested in Redglare's story when he described a knife which he knew Steve usually carried.

A detective asked him to draw it — and Redglare's picture showed the long knife with a black jaguar carved on the handle, which police believe is the murder weapon.

Rockets says he knew Sid and Nancy for about a month and had occasionally provided them with Dilaudid — a synthetic morphine which is used to treat cancer patients.

He claims that at 1.30 on the morning of Nancy's death he received a phone call from her offering to buy 40 pills at £20 each.

He added: "I told her I didn't have that kind of money to get the pills. But she said: 'Don't worry, we've got the money here'."

He told detectives he went to the couple's room in the run-down Chelsea Hotel, and was with them until 4 am.

He saw a wad of 100-dollar bills fall out of Nancy's purse.

Police interviewed Redglare for nine hours.

They are wary of his story in case he is trying to protect Vicious, now recovering from self-inflicted wounds in the psychiatric ward of a New York hospital.

Private

But they have admitted that there are several independent factors which make the account credible.

And Vicious's lawyer, Mr James Merberg said yesterday: "I have sent a private investigator to interview Rockets Redglare at length."

Rolling Stone magazine, which originally interviewed Redglare, said it was common knowledge at the Chelsea Hotel that Sid and Nancy carried large sums of money with them.

One tenant in the seedy rooming house recalled seeing Nancy drop several dollar bills on the floor of the lobby while paying her rent —and not even bothering to pick them up.

Cash

Sid's manager, Malcom McClaren, sent him a large cheque which arrived the day before Nancy died.

And Sid had also just collected £1,500 in cash for four performances in the States.

Yet when detectives entered the room Nancy's purse was open and empty on top of a dresser.

Some of Sid's most prized possessions — including his leather jacket and two Sex Pistols gold records — were later found in another bedroom occupied by a punk rocker.

Vicious has always maintained he knew nothing about Nancy's death.

He says he woke up in the morning to find her naked body in the bathroom.

Detectives say that the robbery—if there was a robbery — could not automatically be linked to the murder.

It could have been committed by any of the hotel's inhabitants who got word of Nancy's death before police were called in.

But they have now widened the scope of their investigations.

One feature of the murder has always puzzled the police.

Strange

The ambulance was called by someone claiming to be Vicious using the New York emergency code—911.

Tenants of the hotel say it is unlikely that an Englishman in a strange city, waking from a drug trip, would have remembered the number.

They claim someone else made that phone call.

Nancy . . . naked and dead in the bathroom

Sid weeps in court drama

From CHRISTOPHER BUCKLAND in New York

THE tough-guy image of punk rocker Sid Vicious crumbled last night as he broke down and sobbed in his mother's arms.

Tuesday, October 24, 1978

I want to join Nancy, says Sid Vicious

From LESLIE HINTON in New York

SEX PISTOLS punk star Sid Vicious tried to commit suicide yesterday—and said he wanted to join his dead girl friend, Nancy Spungen.

Vicious, who is on bail accused of her murder, slashed wildly at his arms with a razor and a broken light bulb.

Then he tried to hurl himself from an eighth-floor hotel window in New York—as his sobbing mother, Anne Beverly, looked on in horror.

Vicious "a death bargain"

PLANNED

He was stopped by his psychiatrist. Later Vicious, blood pouring from both arms, told friends:

"I want to die. I want to join Nancy. I didn't keep my part of the bargain

Nancy Spungen: I take a lot of brandy. Pour a small one for Sid and a large one for me. Sid's not supposed to drink. Otherwise he'll die. ***(4/2/78).***

Bitter blow for Vicious

SID VICIOUS' fight to raise the £25,000 to fund his court battle against the charge of murdering his girlfriend, Nancy Spungen, is in serious trouble after the Sex Pistol was back in jail charged with assaulting a musician.

SID: The first to go in 1979

SID VICIOUS: "I'll die before I'm very old."

THE DEATH of Sid Vicious, from a heroin overdose, on Friday comes as no great surprise.

21 year old Sid had been struggling with heroin addiction since the height of his notoriety with the Sex Pistols and at one time had been running a £40 a day habit. He had tried to break the habit several times but had slipped back -- until he was taken into custody in New York, charged with murdering his girlfriend Nancy Spungen. In prison, doctors had kept him on a methedone course -- the drug used to alleviate withdrawal symptoms -- and they think that by cleaning out his body, his usual dose of heroin would have been lethal. Sid died after a party thrown to celebrate his release from prison on bail.

It wasn't the first time Sid collapsed in the States. At the end of the abortive Pistols' tour in 1977, Sid became ill on a flight from the West Coast and was taken to hospital in New York. He said then that he'd taken an accidental overdose. His dependance on the drug built up from there.

"Nancy and me used to ride around in cabs for hours trying to raise money to buy drugs," Sid told me last Easter. "Sometimes we'd just inject cold water, just to get the buzz of seeing the blood and the needle going in. We had needle fixation."

Nancy, who'd been an addict for three years, told me: "Fixing was almost sexual, almost orgasmic, but it was awful."

Both prophesised the early deaths. "I'll die before I'm very old," Sid told me. "I don't know why, I just have this feeling . . ."

Nancy agreed and added: "I'll kill myself as soon as the first wrinkle appears. I don't want to grow old and lose my looks."

Nancy was found in a seedy New York hotel bedroom last October, with a hunting knife rammed in her stomach. Although Sid was charged with the murder, there were conflicting reports about a so called "admission" and later Sid denied the charge.

Certainly when I interviewed the pair, they seemed crazy about each other and Sid told me Nancy was the only woman he'd ever cared about. He said she was a restraining influence on his bouts of violence.

"I used to fight a lot more," said Sid, "but now I'm with Nancy I can't, because she can't run as fast as me and I can't leave her behind."

Sid's reputation for violence was well charted and admitted to me that the nickname Vicious was deserved.

"At school I got in fights every day. I just liked the feeling of mashing someone up and splitting them open."

His mother, Mrs Ann Beverley, maintains that Sid was really a good boy, but his own version was different.

"When I was angry and had no-one else to cut up, I cut myself," he told me. I had more pressure on me than anyone else in the group. I had to play dope-sick a lot of these nights and no-one understood what it was like. But I still managed to play all right, though I was in the worst pain the world. I survived because I was tough."

No tough enough to withstand the no hope life of a heroin addict though. Sid is dead and it's the end of a chapter in rock history -- though Malcolm McLaren still intends to bring out a single of Sid's (while the Sex Pistols' biographers, Fred and Judy Velmoral, also bring out a single, entitled 'Sidney Glittergas', under the name of the Cash Pussies on the Label on February 23) -- and he'll go down as the first rock and roll death of '79. Some distinction. ROSALIND RUSSELL.

"We started to get huge orders for Nigeria, so we looked into it a little bit and it became clear that something extraordinary was happening there, that reggae had suddenly become a massive new fad. So that's when Richard went off on his trip to

Jamaica

with suitcases stuffed full of money, to sign up as many reggae artists as possible. Then we started the Front Line label, as much as anything, just to be able to put all of this material out, so that it didn't flood Virgin. We had acres of it, and in the end we were chartering jumbo jets to take all of these records out to Nigeria. All that seemed to stop. It was: a) maybe the market was being flooded; and, perhaps more to the point, b) there was a military coup, and they stopped all imports."

S.D.

No strangers to wind direction, the hard-hitting Virgin team immediately targeted Nigeria as their initial market of choice and promptly inundated the proud little overeign nation with two million LPs featuring various exponents of the Tosh persuasion — causing corporate cash flow to take a decidedly positive turn .. . until a so-called *coup d'état* (or "crazy mix-up" as Virgin top staffers characterized it) brought the jackpot payout to an abrupt, and some would say disastrous, end. "It was actually quite sticky," commented one director of the board. "If you garner my inference, in point of fact, we had to start looking for tall cotton, and pronto!"

"I wanna sing to de world, mon. I want de people to dance but at de same time I want de black people to get de message. Most black music, all dosé discotheque music, is just . . . get down, get down . . . but my music is get up 'cos we bin down too long mon."

M.M. 13.11.'76

U-Roy is as important to Jamaica as the Beatles are to Britain. The whole "sound system" cult, skanking, and dee-jay communication followed in his wake.

N.M.E. 3.5.78

"You have a certain number of people really love me, y'know. Anywhere me sing them go swing."

U-ROY

We work super-quick,"
oseph smiles. "Is no
ieed for a brother to sit
lown and t'ink, ''Ow is it
Culture get through songs
o fast?' It is because
ve 'ave our t'ing"
he clicks his fingers –
'so-o-o-o strong.
Everbody's spirit
s well equipped."

NME 3.6.78

rankin' trevor

"We are the music makers
from Jamaica. We come
with the intention to mash
it down, and tonight we are
going to wrench it up."

THE GLADIATORS
AT THE 100 CLUB, 27.5.78

"All of us are builders, we used to work together – the music start right on the job. Bringing the guitar along from I was a man who love guitar, and going along the line and finding that I have friends beside me, we start to sit down at nights and just keep singing till it keep vibrating outta me head. Then we really decide and say, well bwoy, we can give it a try because I have a feeling that we could really make it."

ALBERT GRIFFITHS

the mighty diamonds

"Our songs now relate to people and world feelings. It no deal with no individuals, just the world and who the cap fits."

TABBY DIAMOND

the twinkle brothers

"Is a good place for us to record, Kingston, although some of the members of the group don't like it – too much hustle. When we was recording there, the people were stealing the food from lorries that were left there to unload into the shops, so there was a curfew and policemen everywhere. We were being stopped and searched on our way to the studios. Is the right atmosphere to make rebel music."

NORMAN GRANT,
THE TWINKLE BROS.

"Their geographical location has contributed to a distinctly different sound and to their lack of recorded work. A range of mountains divides the north coast from Kingston in the south, where all the influential studios are. Getting down there for them is not easy. I'm a DJ of many voices. Sometimes I talk as a sixteen-year-old. Sometimes I sound as a ninety-year-old. It depends on the content of the lyrics."

PRINCE HAMMER

"I'm a man, right? I got a concept. I got a morality. I got a culture. I know right from wrong. Everyone is in this world to give, an' what I'm givin' to people is words of wisdom, of love, of encouragement. And I 'ave never suffered from a barren intuition. It's the concept, the cleanness of your 'eart. If you are dealin' with righteousness, 'ow can you fight a man?"

I-ROY

"Yu wiggle an yu wine everyday. Christopher Columbus discover America, but I discover music."
PRINCE FAR-I

BIG YOUTH: Dread Locks Dread: Front Line FL1014

THIS album is a stone delight. Its like watching Bela Lugosi beckoning some hapless victim in a Sunday afternoon B horror movie.

Big Youth is so unlike any other DJ. All the talk you hear nowadays about it being impossible to listen to a toasting album all the way through just doesn't apply to this man.

M.M. 4.10.'78

ABBYSINIANS: "I and I"/"Satta Massa Gana" (Different). Produced by Clive Hunt.

No nonsense. H-a-a-r-m-o-n-y...terra incognita vocals, outaspace way, Abbysinians style. The prime contenders for Reggae vocal group supreme (not as diverse as Manhattan Transfer or The King Singers but with lotsa talent) – these two sides are notable examples of their nonpareil vocals. Especially "I and I" which has a stiff block of maka riddim to assist the voice proceedings – the song itself is good too. "Satta Massa Gana" probably needs no intro from me to you. A worthy hymn that will probably go down in the annals of JA MUSICAL HISTORY. (Rank +++++)

Black Echoes 7.10.78

ALTHEA AND DONNA bounce back with **"Going to Negril"** which has much in common with "Uptown Top Ranking." There's the same shuffling beat, their vocals are cool and hip, the brass is subdued and subtle, and they make a few sexy shrieks to punctuate the number. Full of fun and charm (Virgin Front Line).

HARTLEPOOL MAIL 14.10.78

"I had a fantasti time on that tri to Jamaica, me some wonderfu people, and eve though no-on was really tha interested i appearing on 'To of the Pops,' w signed, I thin some great acts.'

R.

culture

the mighty diamonds

u roy

-ankin' trevor

tapper roote

"**The police** don't know 'oo I am. But they terrorise me. They even take me off the street and lock me up for a few days and terrorise me. I don't carry a gun. **My mouth is my gun.**"

Tappa Zukie

"I remember first of all sitting outside Peter Tosh's house for a day and then sitting inside his house for a day trying to persuade him to sign with us — and I can't remember the end of either day, but I remember he had this huge box of ganja on each occasion.

"Sometimes I think that with British Airways it's become like taking on a bleeding competition with someone who owns a bloodbank; with Peter Tosh it was a slight variation on a similar theme."

R.B.

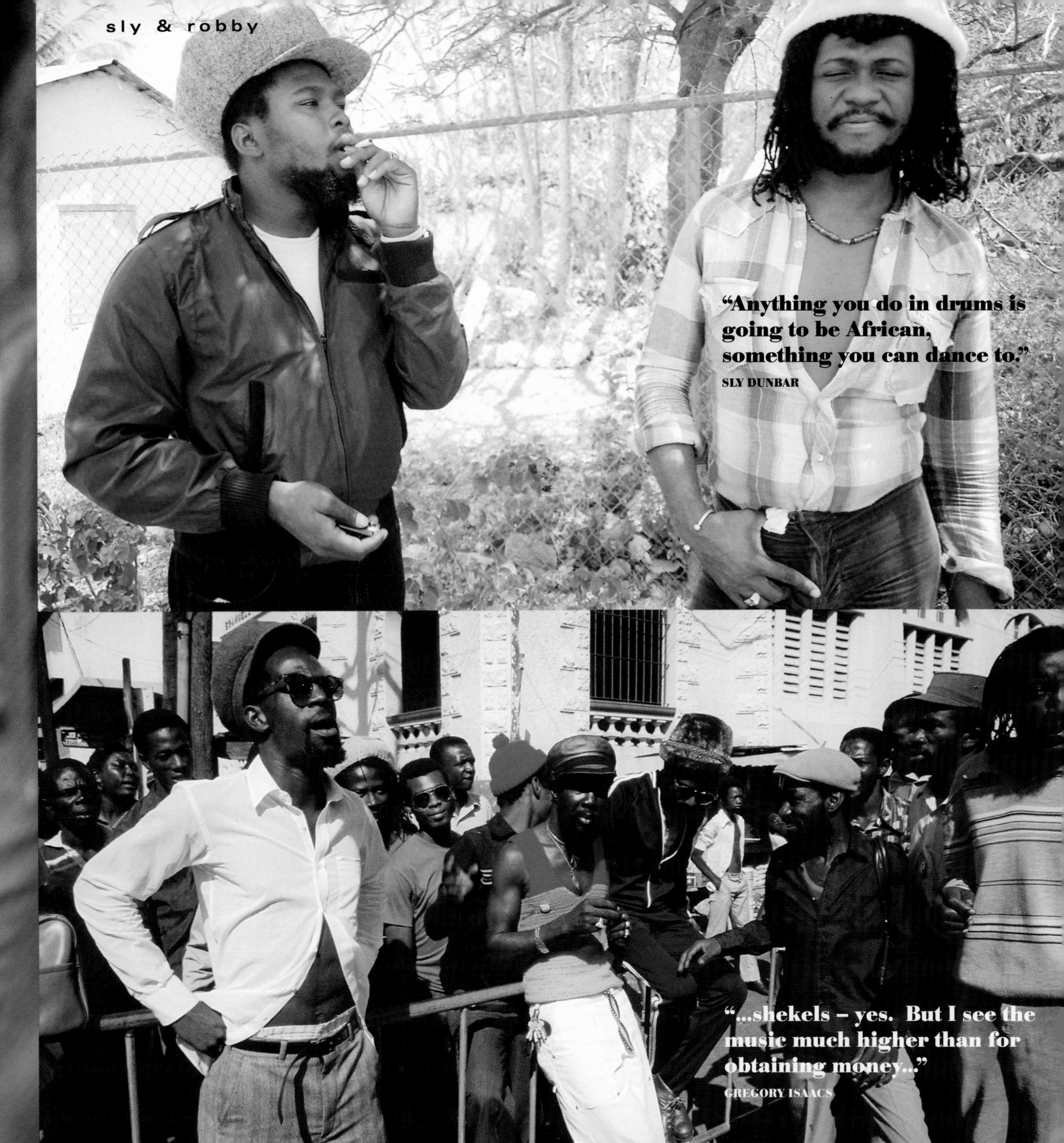

"Anything you do in drums is going to be African, something you can dance to."

SLY DUNBAR

"...shekels – yes. But I see the music much higher than for obtaining money..."

GREGORY ISAACS

"I is a true man that live at a certain 'eight in life, seen? Nothing too really surprise I on earth, because I know what the earth is like. You know the music can be acceptable amongst *all* the population – don't care what colour or creed or race I deal with... *I-niversal*."

"It was really the early '80s when we truly hit it. That was when the whole thing again took another quantum jump. Mainly through Ian Gillan, Phil Collins, Japan, Human League, Boy George, Simple Minds... It was the first time for us that we really had big, big-selling albums worldwide on a consistent basis – not just one or two a year, but a whole load of them.

"Ian Gillan was important to Virgin because he really kicked off all of this success. In 1980 we had to move somewhat swiftly from being terribly idealistic and serious about everything we did to realising, backs to the wall, we've got to sell some records. No one had the remotest interest in heavy metal, but Ian Gillan's manager came to see me, and I said simply, 'Look, we need someone to sell some records!' ...And the funny thing was that after we'd signed him and everyone started to work with him they all liked him. Their attitude changed again and just because he was so great, his own personality swung it.

"Along this same view of having to sell records, I had a meeting with the staff and said, 'No salary rises next year unless we have a platinum album.' The next thing that happened of course was that we did exactly that with Phil Collins.

"Some of the signings actually went back a bit, because I'd signed the Human League in '78, and that was great because they were on their third album when they broke in '82. The previous two hadn't sold a hell of a lot, and I remember going to see them at a stage where they almost looked like they'd just about had it. I was under a lot of pressure from the accountants at Virgin to drop them, when they performed a concert at the Hammersmith Odeon which was two-thirds full. There was a reception afterwards which was a pretty desultory affair. We were trying hard and they'd been quite good but terribly off-key, singing and everything. The two guys who'd formed Heaven 17 had gone. They'd given up after two albums, so this was also after they'd recorded their third record, and Charlie Gillett came up to me and said, 'You know, that band is going to be huge.' That guy truly knows his stuff, even in surprising areas where people might think he doesn't have any expertise, and in the case of Human League, he was the only person who said that to me, and I was able to say to him, 'I know – I know they're going to happen!' I could see what the first two albums were doing. Every week you're looking at sales figures, and usually you get this tail-off. But those albums were starting to pick up – they were starting to sell a thousand a month of

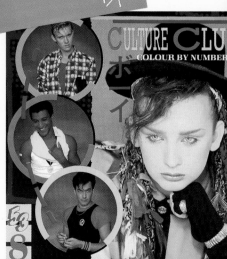

reproduction stuff, so we knew that something was going on.

"The other factor that gave me a big clue concerning what was about to happen was Japan. I'd signed them, I suppose, thinking that they might turn into a young version of Roxy Music, even though they'd already made two or three albums without any great success to speak of. We were launching the album they did for us, however, which was called *Gentlemen Take Polaroids*, and had arranged one concert (because that's all they could manage at the time) to use as a promotional gig when the venue manager asked me for two and a half grand as a subsidy for this one-off show at the Lyceum.

"As we were about to put it up as an additional advance, about three weeks before the performance, the manager rang up again and said, 'I don't want the money anymore.' I said, 'What!' And he said, '**We don't want the money.** We're going to sell this concert out. We could sell it out three times over.' And it's amazing – it's kind of a grass-roots feeling, but that's when I knew that Japan were going to be absolutely huge. Even at Virgin, when I signed them, no one wanted to know; everyone was appalled. Keith Bourton was given Japan because none of the other press officers would touch it. He took their previous albums back home with him over the weekend and, I remember this was another good sign, because he came back on Monday and he was suddenly on to it! Finally! Then we had a silver album with them right off and then the next one was just gold. We got in whether by luck or judgment at the very beginning of the whole glam-rock thing.

"Then came Culture Club, Simple Minds, and onwards and upwards, but really, in the very early '80s it was Ian Gillan, the Human League, Japan, and Phil Collins that turned us around – and none of them were particularly popular signings. I mean it was, '**Phil Collins, who's he?** He's the drummer from Genesis, for Christ's sake!'"

S. D.

ken berry

prince tony

simon draper

Pictured here presenting two gold disks to the manager/promoter Prince Tony, Ken Berry, with several reservations, and after extracting a few pledges re-curbing certain aspects of their personal behavior, had been pursuaded by Branson and Draper to move up in the company to the time-honored position of third wheel.

"Rock music for me is so physical it's not true ... if I'm not crawling away on my hands and knees after a gig, then I haven't done it right."

IAN GILLAN

"Call me fat and I'll rip your spine out."
IAN GILLAN

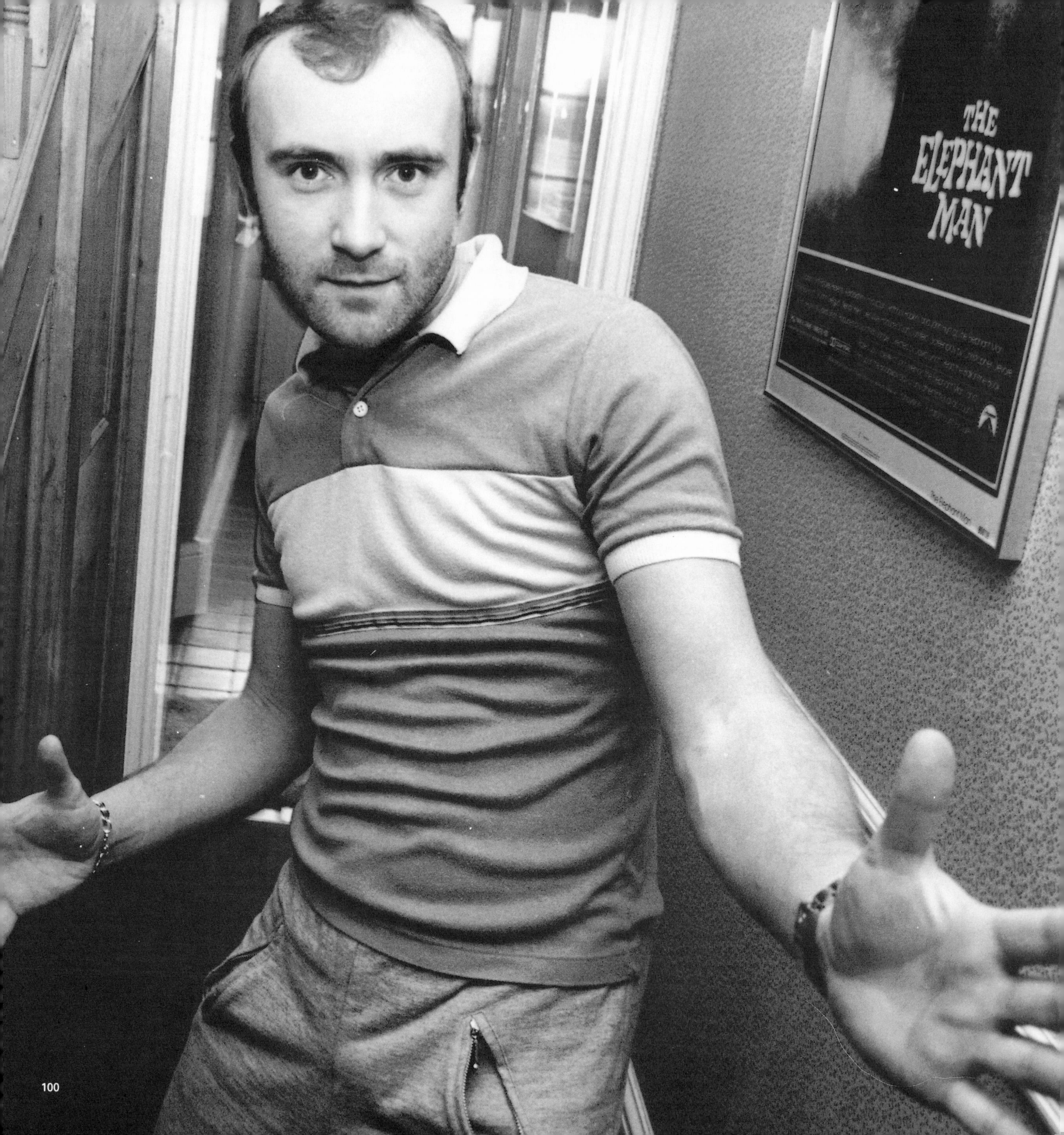
THE ELEPHANT MAN

“I was on ‘60 MINUTES’ and I said that the only musician I’d be absolutely sure of recognizing in a big crowd was **Phil Collins.** The day after I said it, I was in a taxi, and the cabby wouldn’t stop talking. He kept jabbering on and on and told me his mum was a huge fan of mine and could we possibly divert for just a few minutes to pop by and say hello. Of course, it was Phil Collins, **dressed as a taxi driver,** and I didn’t recognize him for the whole of this half-hour journey. He and Peter Gabriel are delightful people. (Damnation – Nothing puts me off so much as an excess of the old suck-hole. Ed.) Nothing’s too much trouble for them, and it’s also true that because they’d both bother to go into the office to see everyone, the staff would just work their balls off for them.”

R.B.

"DEVO.

We had another fun court case with Devo. After they'd signed with us, **Warner Bros.** decided that they already had a verbal agreement with them, so they took us to court. Their lawyer cited a case from 1934 where **Bette Davis** had been successfully prevented from working because it was claimed that she made a living in other ways besides acting. Due entirely to this previous ruling, apparently the judge decided in favor of Warner Bros., but the judge who had set the precedent in 1934, which meant that we lost our case, was actually my grandfather! Worse luck! And bad form all around!"

R.B.

"Sometimes, of course, it's the acts you do expect to take off that don't and vice-versa. It's very exciting when it works. I remember with **Sparks,** we tried terribly hard, spent a fortune trying to promote this record that eventually was a Top Ten song – but it was 9 weeks after the single came out. I mean, now singles come and go in about two weeks (even then nine weeks was a long time). It had been in the charts but rather low and hadn't made it when 'Mike Mansfield,' one of the two television shows that had been booked in very early on and that we couldn't get the timing right for, went out on air. I don't think Sparks were even there. It was just a backing track for the dancers. No one at the company was paying any attention the night the show went out because we thought the record was over. But literally the next day, we were flooded with telephone calls from shops wanting stock, and it just suddenly took off and was a **big, big hit.** I mean, it had nothing to do with anything really, but of course we took a lot of credit for it."

S.D.

The Flying Lizards

"A very talented guy who came up with a one-off single that we put out of a song which the Beatles also covered years earlier, "Money." She sang in a terribly gravelly voice with a sort of scratchy backing – in fact I think it's another track that's been used in an ad just recently."

S.D.

CONDIMENTS
BIRDS
CUSTARD

"There is something unwieldy about the name of this new group you've dredged up," R.B. complained to Simon Draper. "You wouldn't say that," replied the Mave, "if you had a better grasp of Marquee values." "But that is precisely what I am talking about!" snapped R.B., not bothering to disguise his impatience. "How in God's great name are we going to get thirty two letters on a marquee - any marquee - and to do the skywriting advert I had in mind would cost a bloody fortune. No, I'm afraid you've put us up queer street this time my lad, and no mistake!" (I'm always amused at the way these top execs can engage in these fierce squabbles and the next moment be working as one, chuckling together over the unscrupulous, monstro leverage buyout of their nearest cor-

“‘Human League’ gave Virgin their first bonafide number one single, ‘Don’t You Want Me.’ After their second album had done very little, I remember we had a meeting to discuss whether we could afford to carry on with various artists and Simon didn’t have a question in his mind about ‘Human League.’ He insisted that they were going to be an extremely big band for us and of course, once again, he was proved absolutely right.”

Japan's first two albums, ***Adolescent Sex*** and ***Obscure Alternatives*** (both 1978), were unabashedly derived from the art-glam of Roxy Music and David Bowie, which, in combo with the then-cute-as-a-button androgynous image, distinguished them to advantage from their punk and new wave counterparts.

"OUR HAIR is similiar and, funnily enough, so is our eye make-up.

We are both blondes but we're not exactly twins. After all, my friend has gone for the two tone look—mostly blonde with dark plum contrasts.

We use the same eye-make-up technique. Every morning the eye liner goes on to make the eyes look bigger. And, of course everyone wears mascara these days. Ours is blue-black and tear-proof.

In fact we could be sisters . . . if he wasn't a fella!"

David Sylvian

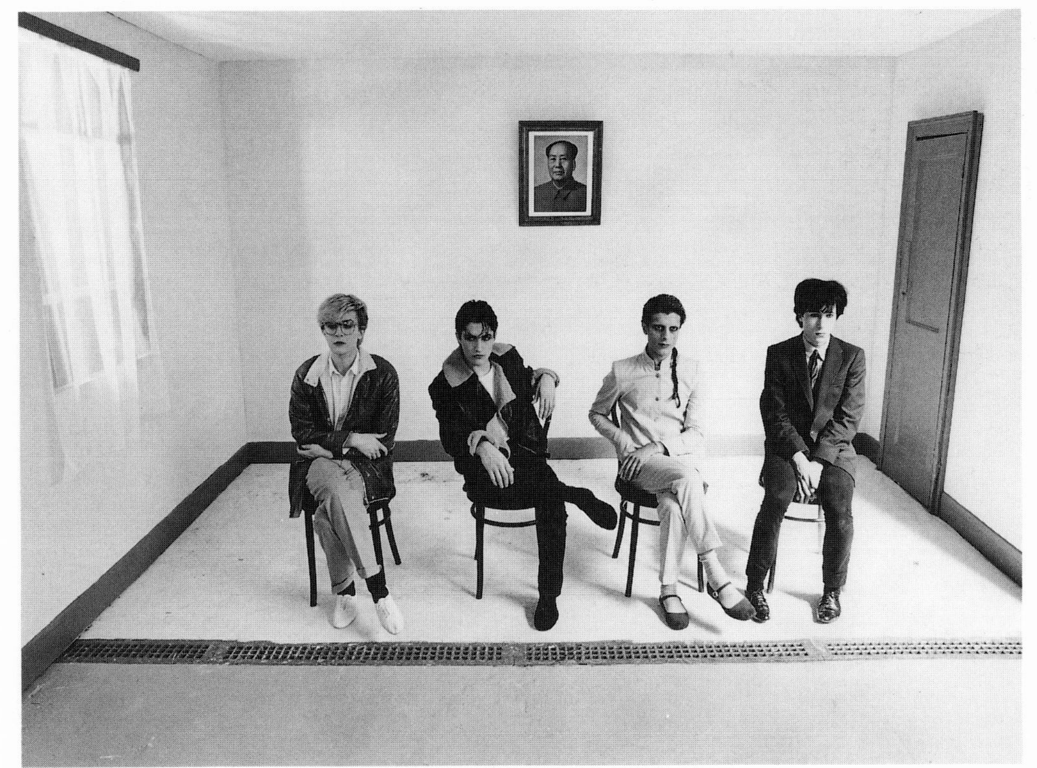

"I was going to be a leader.

I led a street gang called the Black Saints who ruled over seven blocks in Boston – and we were criminals, I guess.

I knew I was going to be a leader – a real one-man dynamo.

I was a natural leader, I was the Godfather, the receiver of stolen goods. The junkies all came to my place.

My mother used to send priests 'round to try to talk me back to the straight and narrow.

I decided to be a pimp because pimps are flamboyant and flashy. I'm slim and attractive. I had a lot of overheads – you gotta impress the new recruits. Pimping is not unlike the music business."

PRINCE CHARLES

Mondo bandage

"Nash the Slash only ever showed his mouth in public."

S.D.

"I'm a good old hard rocker who happens to be doing it in an incredibly weird way. I define my music as Acid Classical."

NASH THE SLASH

"I'm not really bothered about being a superstar overnight or anything like that. I am more concerned with earning some credibility and respect."

JANE AIRE

The excess of the Rotten/Vicious brand of punk was bound to chill itself out in the end, in the way a scorpion threatened with fire will plunge its deadly stinger into its head. Fans and record buyers were finally so on edge and unnerved by the relentless quality of the punk experience, that it is perhaps understandable that they would embrace the new wave of romantics, personified, so some would say, by the stylish scream of Cabaret Voltaire.

Tom Verlaine – Shades of Ingmar, Jr.?

"The pre-Christian poets are the ones who interest me. The one that really caught me – I don't know if I have this straight – was a legend that a real poet had the ability to rhyme rats to death!"

TOM VERLAINE

An exciting blend of funk, freeform jazz and a dash of good old avant-garde from a highly-regarded new outfit that features a couple of old Pop Group members plus peripheral personnel like Ari-Up of the Slits and jazzman Don Cherry's daughter Neneh. God, two lengthy 12" 45s – rather than the more usual single 33-er – is far from easy listening and occasionally attempts far more than it's capable of achieving. But it's by and large a brave and successful stab at synthesising a new dance form from a right old musical cocktail of genres. I'd love to see 'em live.

SOUNDS 18.7.82

Fast food orgy ends with Larry in hospital

Staff at the King Charles Hotel watched aghast as Larry tucked into a midday breakfast of two steaks, two pancakes, eggs and spinach washed down with Bacardi and Coke.

"An hour later he was hungry again so we gave him scrambled eggs and cheeseburgers," says deputy manager Steve Degiorgio. "He went on to hamburger and chips followed by chocolate gateau and ice-cream, washed down with more Bacardi.

"He then had another cheeseburger and more scrambled eggs followed shortly afterwards by a dinner of trout, chips and peas.

"Our cook was able to rest when he went off to give a concert, but the man was hungry when he got back.

"He ate two more cheeseburgers, then took a portion of chips up to bed."

Between meals, Larry took repeated baths where he meditated and made funny noises.

Shortly afterwards he collapsed and was rushed to hospital.

"He is suffering from bronchial trouble," said an aide.

DAILY MIRROR 2.11.82

"Although modeling was fun, we were getting bored. We wanted to do something that would stretch our minds more."

KATY LYNNE, GIRLS CAN'T HELP IT

Two contemporary singers who might truly be called fantastic are Tiny Tim and Boy George. But there the comparison ends. Tiny Tim sings in a melodic falsetto; Boy George sings in a non-vibrato tenor – sweet, musical and very powerful. His group, **Culture Club**, played their first gig in October '81 and signed to Virgin six months later. But it was not until their third single, the reggae-tinged "Do You Really Want to Hurt Me," that they reached the ever-lucky Number One in the U.K. Top Ten and Number Two in the U.S. of A.

I consider myself fortunate indeed to have heard the "Boy George story" from the wise old man who found and succoured the unfortunate lad, none other than Simon "the Mave" Draper. "It is a story," he said, as we snuggled in near the cozy hearth of the Sow and Merkin, "which could bring tears from the stone. After his success with "Do You Really Want to Hurt Me,' Boy George found himself alone and vulnerable – sudden fame is so often like that, isn't it? An easy prey for the notorious shooters from Brooklyn Heights, the poor boy was soon consuming drugs through his every bodily orifice, and all the while pleading for more! It soon became the scandal of the music industry and of great interest to the entire Great British Public. The newspapers would not let it rest. *'Don't Break Your Poor Mum's Heart!'* said THE EVENING MAIL; *'Britain Needs You!'* said THE TELEGRAPH; and a simple *'Please!'* from THE MIRROR. " Finally, the dear boy's parents came down to London and went on breakfast television with a personal and tearful plea, followed by the evening's headlines: ***'Come In, Boy George.'*** " Mr. Draper paused in his narrative and had a sip from his tall one. "Ah, yes," he went on, "and quite the rave-up we had when we got him back in the fold, I don't mind telling you."

"Boy George just had everything you could possibly want in a star- he looked great, sang great, he wrote great songs, he was determined to be successful, he stood out from the crowd and was an absolutely brilliant signing by Simon. Then I think that even though George is very bright, intelligent and articulate the success that he had was so tremendous and happened so quickly really that he just couldn't completely cope with it and he fell into drugs. So whether you run a record company or whether you're a friend, I think that if somebody's ill with drugs you have to do what you can in that situation, and because we've run an advisory centre since I was a teenager and knew roughly how to help someone come off drugs, which isn't easy,I thought I'd do my best to try to help to get him clean again. One of the remarkeable things that happened, however, was that I think the press almost bullied the police into arresting George when he was right in the middle of a course of recovery. I mean I'm not sure that people should be arrested when their taking drugs anyway, it's an illness and perhaps not something which should be a criminal offence- but when somebody is trying so hard to get off drugs and they have a doctor helping them through that process, to arrest them in that situation is, I think, very wrong. The point with something LIKE HEROIN, however, is that it's possible to get through it and thank God, George has done exactly that, is well again now and very, very strong."

R.B.

KiBOcol

"I use the medium of juju music to preach what I believe in: Christ and love. To begin with, I played I. K. Dairo style, but it didn't really work, so I started my own sound, Miliki system. It means 'enjoyment.'"

Chief Ebeneezer Obey

Super Mazemebe Orchestra limber up in Kenya.

"...There is a tremendous resistance among the British record-buying public to anything not sung in English, unless it's Julio Iglesias. It's the foreign-holiday syndrome. We expect everybody to speak our language. And that is the big problem African music will face."

JEREMY LASCELLES,
(Top Virgin staffer of the day)

One of the grandest industry coups of the "Fab Mave" (as he is frequently called) occurred when he persuaded the mammoth French record company EMI to "lend" Virgin two of their mega stars, the SRO Sinatra-style pop singer, Julian Clerc, and the Top of the Charts French rock group Telephone, referred to as "the biggest thing in France since DeGaulle's great schnoz." (M.M. 8.83) The plan was that the two groups would trip over to England, knock off a couple of tracks, and back to fair France in "double quick" order. "In with the tide, out with the tide, and none the wiser" was how the Mave and Dick Branson explained it to EMI execs. As fate would have it, however, the two stars from EMI found the atmosphere at Virgin so relaxed and pleasant, and the people so free-wheeling, and so *très sympa* that they just stayed on indefinitely. It all worked out in the end, however, when EMI, in a fit of pique over the loss of their megas, simply purchased the other company outright. I happened to overhear Branson and Draper discussing it later. "I find myself wondering," Dick Branson said, "if there isn't possibly a scintilla of bad form involved in this whole affair." "Hold on, Dick," cautioned the Mave, "I never said we could make an omelette without breaking a few eggs."

telephone

"What started us off in France was that EMI U.K. wouldn't release **Telephone** or **Julian Clerc**'s albums in the U.K., so we went to EMI and said we would like to release the records. So they licensed their own act to Virgin! **We got to know them**, they got to know us, and literally when their next album deals were up, who did they sign with? They signed with us, but for France as well as for the U.K. – and that EMI couldn't believe. In the world of record companies, it was unheard of."

S.D.

Regarding **Holly Beth Vincent** of Holly & the Italians, Mave Draper had this to say: "She's no mere bit of fluff." (Aye, not by half in my view. **34-24-34,** if my guess is any good, and every ounce Grade A prime, if you garner my indication. Ed.) "I experienced only mild surprise therefore," the Mave continued, "when the comely lass went on to write such particularly apt gems as **'Better Be Good to Me,'** which of course Tina Turner put across in 1986 with such mega-huge style on her album *Private Dancer*."

WORLD'S
FAMOUS
SUPREME
TEAM

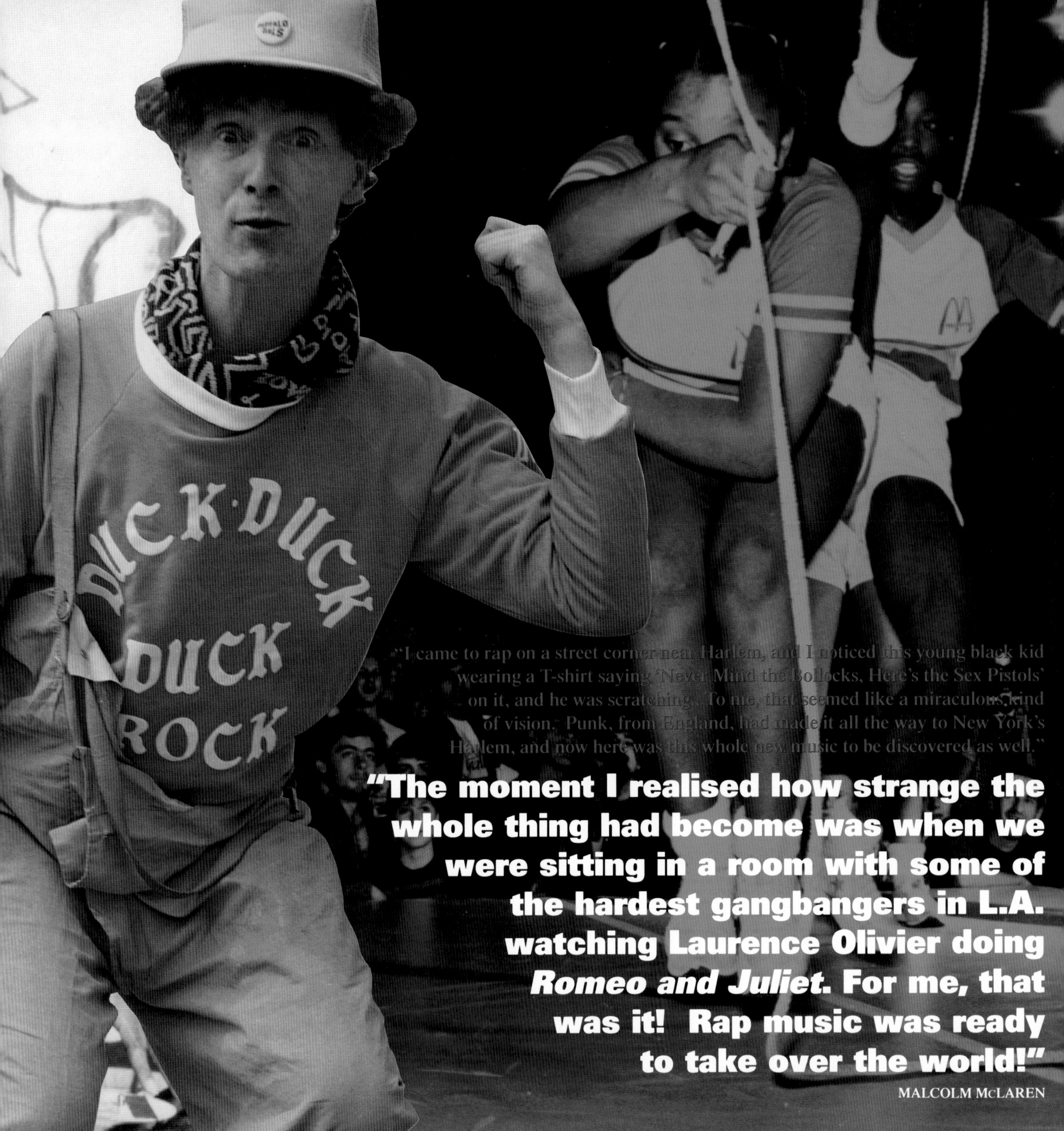

"I came to rap on a street corner near Harlem, and I noticed this young black kid wearing a T-shirt saying 'Never Mind the Bollocks, Here's the Sex Pistols' on it, and he was scratching. To me, that seemed like a miraculous kind of vision. Punk, from England, had made it all the way to New York's Harlem, and now here was this whole new music to be discovered as well."

"The moment I realised how strange the whole thing had become was when we were sitting in a room with some of the hardest gangbangers in L.A. watching Laurence Olivier doing *Romeo and Juliet*. For me, that was it! Rap music was ready to take over the world!"

MALCOLM McLAREN

Parallel indeed to all the straightforward, no-frills, syncopation on the mean streets of **Harlem, U.S.A.,** an extraordinary bit of weirdness was jumping off. Apparently inspired by **epileptic** seizures, young men had developed a dance which began by flinging themselves to the sidewalk, then gyrating like things possessed. It was as if someone being electrocuted had suddenly fallen out of the chair. It was a highly competitive art form, and the young men went to outlandish lengths to better their opponents. The dance was so rambunctious, so frequently injurious to the practitioner, **that it was called "breakdancing."** Mave Simon liked the spontaneity of the new dance but was at first stymied as to how to "turn it to some readdies." "Then, quite by chance," he recalled, "just outside a rather low doss-house – I was there by the remotest of happenstance, you understand – I came across this lot." He was referring, of course, to the now rather celebrated Rock Steady Crew, one of the earliest and most accomplished devotees of the curious craft. (Whom he signed on the spot. Ed.)

rock steady crew

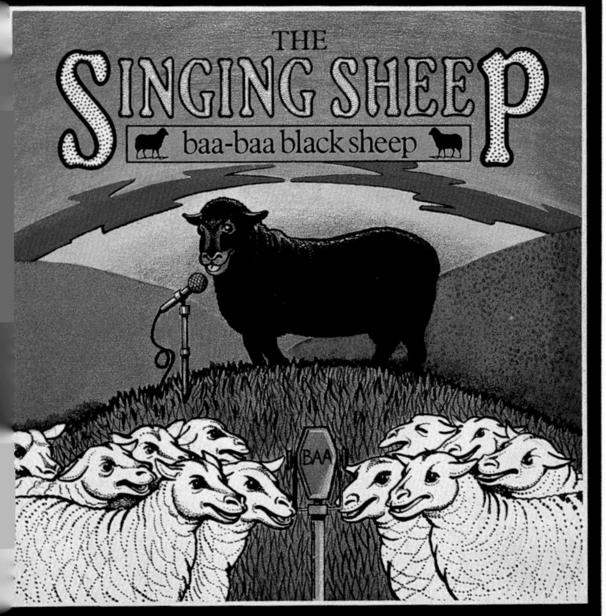

"My aunt, who runs a black sheep farm, telephoned me one day to say she was sure that one of the sheep was singing 'Bah, Bah Black Sheep.' So I sent a 24-track mobile down to record it and, believe it or not, I think it got into the Top Twenty – it was one of those fun one-offs that helped promote my aunt's sheep farm!"

R.B.

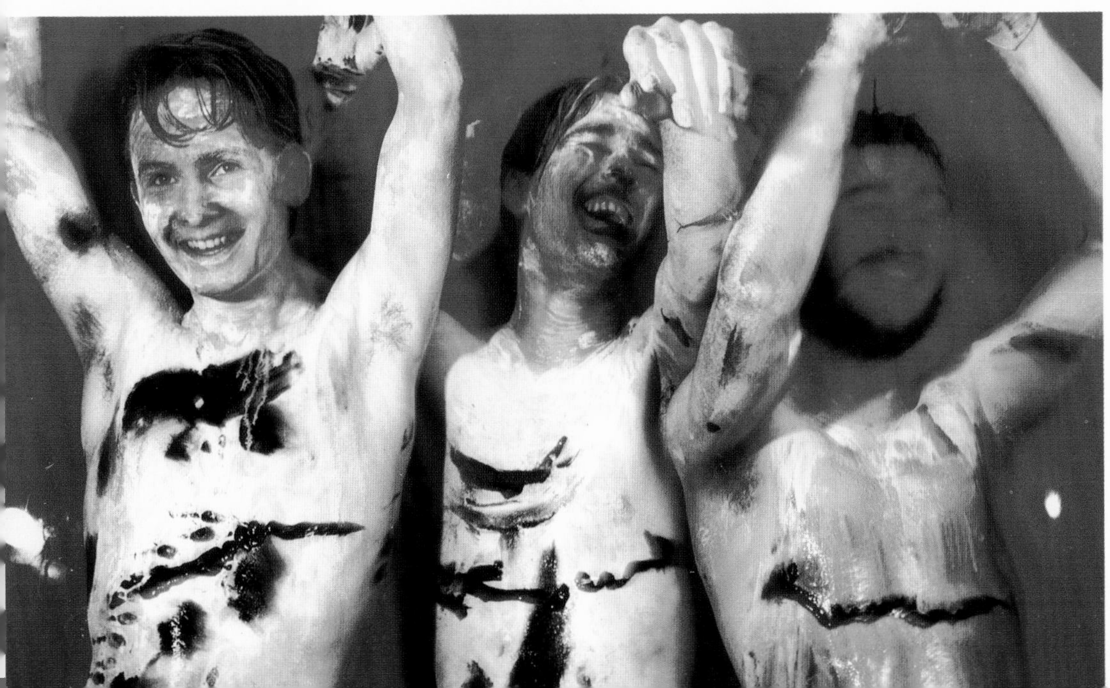

"...One of your main aims if you're only eighteen or nineteen is to actually get your records out. It doesn't matter if it's on fucking Fine Fare: Don't want any money, sing for a packet of crisps — that kind of attitude! But I'm below the poverty line — I'm on £16 a week. We needed some clothes and our manager said, 'I don't know what you do with your money, Gary — I mean, 16 quid!' He's just like a bad dad."

GARY DALY, CHINA CRISIS

FLAKE OFF, QUEEN STA
TELLS DEB
OLD FLAM
SHOWDOWN . . . the dramatic moment when Climie (left), Taylor and Flake girl Debbie clashed
Picture by DAVE HOGAN

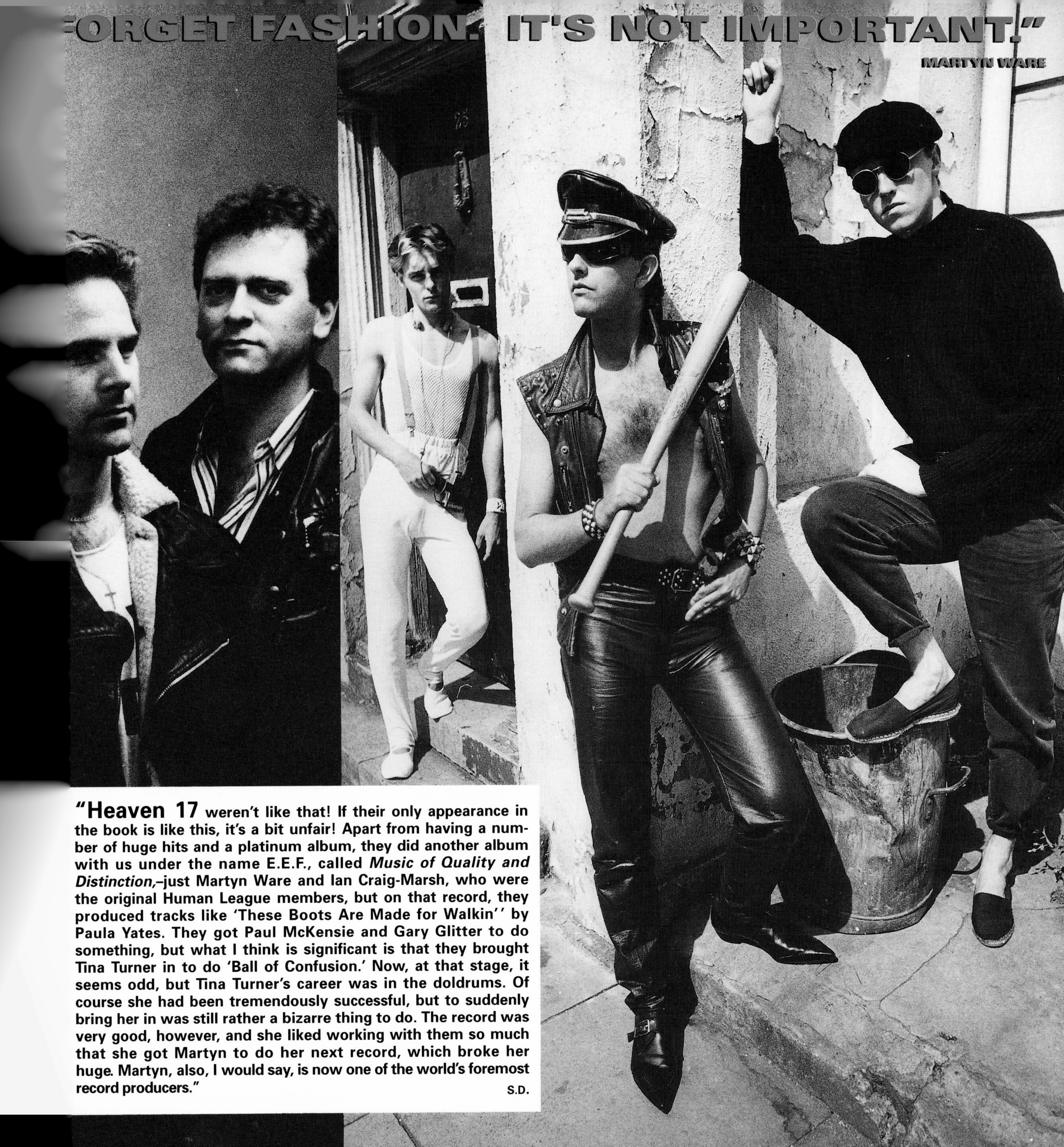

FORGET FASHION. IT'S NOT IMPORTANT."

MARTYN WARE

"Heaven 17 weren't like that! If their only appearance in the book is like this, it's a bit unfair! Apart from having a number of huge hits and a platinum album, they did another album with us under the name E.E.F., called *Music of Quality and Distinction,*–just Martyn Ware and Ian Craig-Marsh, who were the original Human League members, but on that record, they produced tracks like 'These Boots Are Made for Walkin'' by Paula Yates. They got Paul McKensie and Gary Glitter to do something, but what I think is significant is that they brought Tina Turner in to do 'Ball of Confusion.' Now, at that stage, it seems odd, but Tina Turner's career was in the doldrums. Of course she had been tremendously successful, but to suddenly bring her in was still rather a bizarre thing to do. The record was very good, however, and she liked working with them so much that she got Martyn to do her next record, which broke her huge. Martyn, also, I would say, is now one of the world's foremost record producers." S.D.

"Miles Davis recorded one of Scritti Politti's songs. I just heard one of their records again recently and it really struck me that it's pop, but it's classy, it's got jazz. I mean, it's just extraordinary, wonderful stuff."

S.D.

Scared out of their Minds

TOP Scottish rockers 'Simple Minds' fled in horror after coming face-to-face with a Ku-Klux-Klan mob at a gig.

"We all knew we had to get out of there — fast. We made a mad dash for our dressing room and locked the door."

JIM KERR

"The [illegible] come when individual artists from Africa will be able to transcend category as freely and unselfconsciously as any other pop-music performers. That will be a good day for African music, for world music, for music."

YOUSSOU N'DOUR

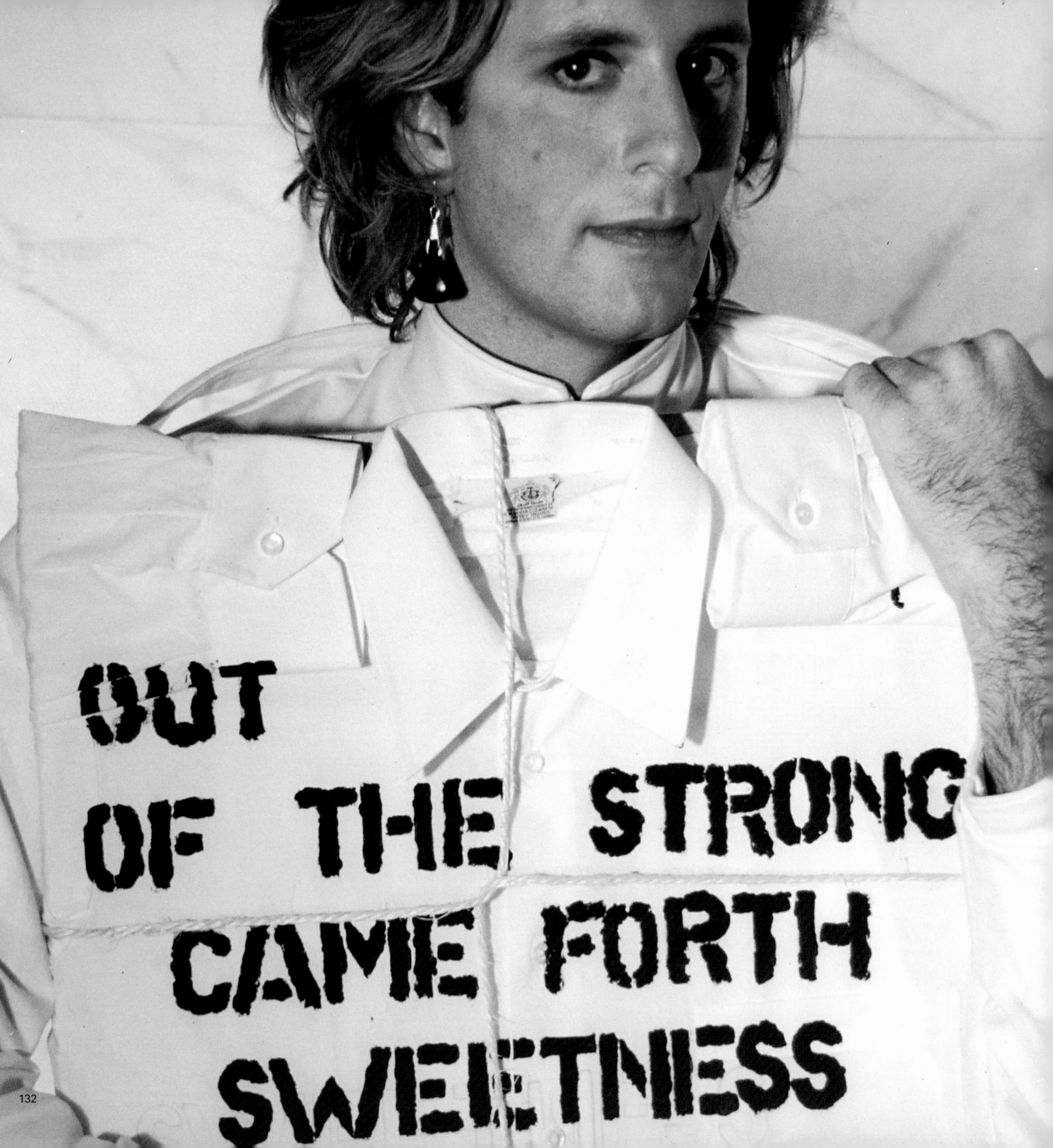

peter green of scritti politti

OUT
OF THE STRONG
CAME FORTH
SWEETNESS

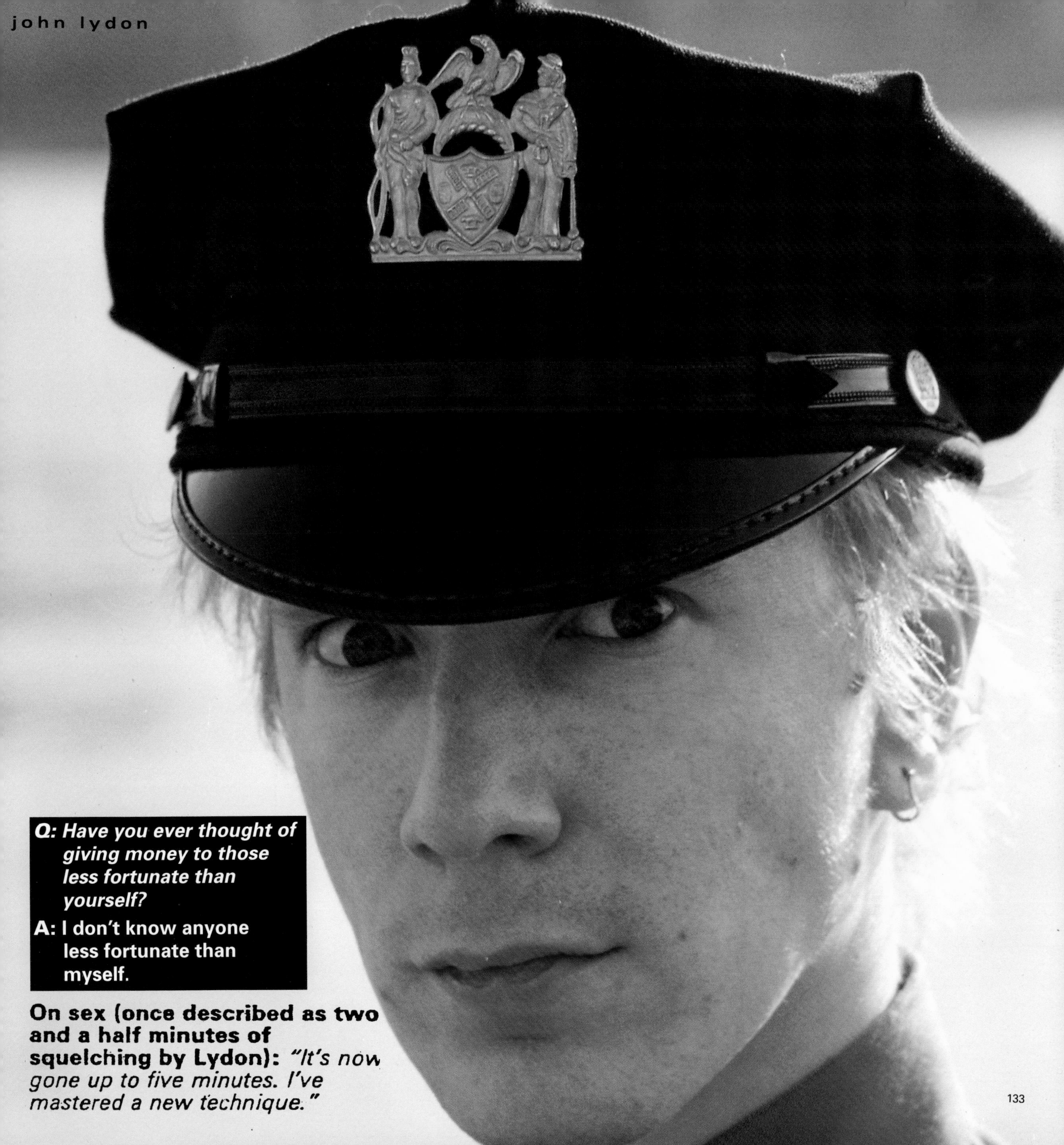

***Q:* Have you ever thought of giving money to those less fortunate than yourself?**

A: I don't know anyone less fortunate than myself.

On sex (once described as two and a half minutes of squelching by Lydon): *"It's now gone up to five minutes. I've mastered a new technique."*

"Richard made us sign **UB40**
at a time when I would have not
signed them, because they looked
like they were going down
when actually they were
just pausing for breath – and,
of course, they turned out to be
an absolutely brilliant signing."

S.D.

"Simon's being very kind and turning a blind eye to a number of suggestions of mine that didn't exactly work out. I just liked the name UB40. Then I went to see them play live in Birmingham and just had a great, fun evening. They were, and still are, an extremely enjoyable and interesting band to watch."

R.B.

MID EIGHTIES

"I'd like to think that Virgin had a plan; I suspect it didn't. There was always a lot going on. I mean, Richard was never one to want to slow down. The record companies were expanding internationally, particularly in Europe and in '84 the airline started, which of course made a big difference to Virgin. Richard adopted for the first time a very high profile to support its launch, which in turn also shifted a lot of focus away from the record shops and the record company. It made the whole operation a broader-based business, which I don't think was either good or bad but was simply part of the organic process which made Virgin what it was then and what it is today. Some people in music were intrigued to see this frenzied activity in diversification, while others simply looked at the merits of Virgin as a music company and liked that, so we attracted artists to the company for a host of different reasons."

K.B.

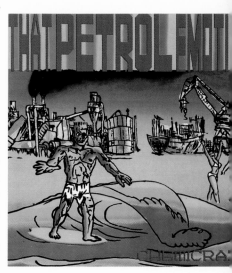

"What I learned from Virgin is that

small is beautiful.

If any company got too big, I would go in and see the deputy managing director, deputy sales manager, deputy marketing manager and say, 'You are now the marketing manager, the sales manager, the managing director of a new company." In that way, we set up a number of subsidiary labels so that even in foreign countries we split the companies up into smaller units, so that people were dealing with individuals of a small company rather than one person who was chairman of a very large company.

"The heads of many of our rival record companies were changing every two years or so. Simon, Ken, and myself had worked together since we were about twenty years old. We balanced each other extremely well, were great friends, and that stability, I think, also gave Virgin its strength.

"Something I decided quite early on, though, was that Virgin needed to be set up in every country around the world, that just giving our artists to somebody else to promote was very frustrating because we might believe in them, but other companies would not necessarily have the same commitment. So, unlike A&M, Island, Chrysalis, and other independents, we set up in seventeen European countries, Japan, Australia, the Far East, and America.

"The first time we opened in America in '79, we really needed instant success, which unfortunately, we didn't have. When we went back a few years later, we knew we had enough strength to do it properly, and you need that staying power because that market can severely cost anyone: You can go a long way down before you come back out again. In fact, I think it was only in '93 that Virgin America really came of its own in a major way."

R.B.

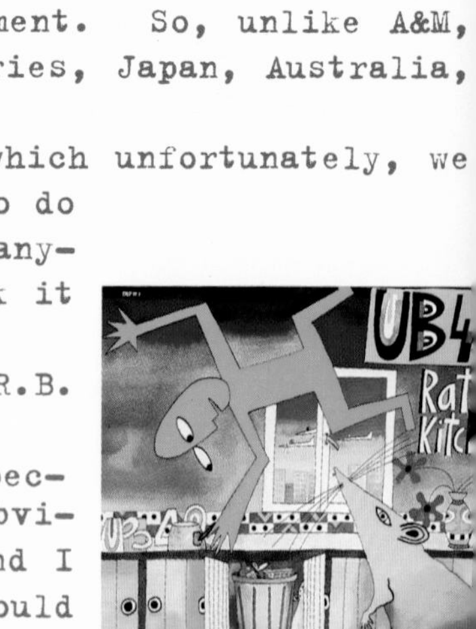

"In '86 we took the Virgin Group public, so suddenly we had to work out what our respective titles were. I mean, we'd never bothered about it up until then, so Richard obviously became the chairman of the Virgin Group, Simon, chairman of Virgin Music, and I was named MD. In practice, however, Simon was also running Virgin U.K. – so he would report to me, and I'd promptly report straight back to him."

K.B.

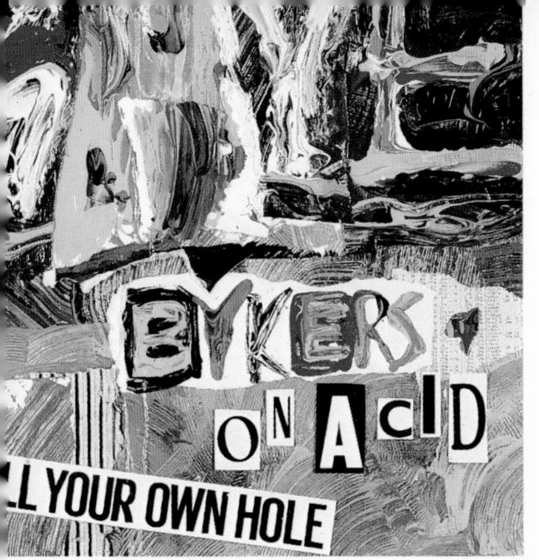

"To me, what made the label work was that you had Richard's unbelievable, exceptional, unusual skills as a publicist and someone who makes things happen. But the rest of us, led by me if you like, were solely into music and making a quality record label. So, really, that was a good battle because he would constantly be trying to get me to sign all kinds of naff groups, and I would be trying to explain to him that, yes, they might be successful, but that's no way to go."

S.D.

A Tiff Between Top Toffs

Quite an amusing *contre-temps* the other p.m. between the twin titans of Virgin Records - Richie Branson and Simon Draper. A rather elaborate "make or break" press conference had been laid on at the ballroom of the Dorchester Hotel - meant to be a sort of "statement of principles" from the fast-growing company. Branson had wanted to "field the questions" but at the last minute agreed that his partner could have the honour. So, when the *Times* correspondent asked what the company's dominant "musical concerns" would be in searching out new talent, Simon Draper, doubly dapper in his new Saville Row finery, stepped smartly to the microphone. "Well," he said, "you see, it's the, how shall I put it...well, the *je ne sais quoi*, if you like...or the plain and simple riz might be more to the point, know what I mean, the old char-riz? Yes? Am I getting through to the GBP? Hello? Hello? Anyone out there?" He cupped his ear towards the puzzled reporters and grimaced oddly, his eyes wide, as in extreme consternation.

Branson was vexed. "I cannot believe you did that," he kept repeating, "simply cannot believe it." "What, what?" Draper wanted to know. "I thought it went off quite well actually."

"Are you mad?" asked Branson. "It was a major, major, high-profile, ruddy balls-up, that's what it was! What in God's great name was that thing about 'riz,' for example?" Draper seemed puzzled, "What, the old char-riz?"

"And what was all that French about?" said Branson. "What was that in aid of, if I may ask?" Draper gave him a straight look and arched his brows. "Just trying to lend a bit of class to the proceedings," he explained. "The British loathe French!" thundered Branson.

"The GBP?" said Draper, with a sniff of vague disdain. This rubbed Dick Branson the wrong way. "Yes!" he fairly shouted. "The bloody GBP! The vast unwashed GBP, in whom we bloody well depend for our own bloody living!" Draper remained unfazed. "I don't believe," he said, "that I've ever heard you express your feelings so...well, so...so *je ne sais quoi*...so, one might almost say, *tout sans finesse*."

"I can tell you the reason for that," snapped Branson, "it is because I have never had to deal with such an utterly bollocksed situation. I mean, what's K.B. going to say? He leaves us alone to run the store for five minutes and straightaway there's a monstrous fuck-up! I still can't believe what happened - I literally feel quite sick about it. And now there's our third wheel to deal with when he gets back." He paused and fixed Mave Draper with a penetrating gaze. "And I expect you, sir, to handle your share of the heat from K.B.!"

madam butterfly

"Oldfield and Virgin Records," said Simon Draper, "are no strangers to the charts--also, we may expect a great deal more of the same in the years to come." (Hear, hear! Ed.)

Tip Top Tone Stratton leads Dick Branson in a merry dance as he explains the advantage of acquiring his record company, **Charisma.** "It will make Virgin a force to be reckoned with in the industry." "I thought he was being rather cheeky at first," said Branson, "but when I looked over his list of new young artists, I thought, What the hell, let's go with the flow, and I made him an offer." (An offer he couldn't refuse, if you glean my indication. Ed.)

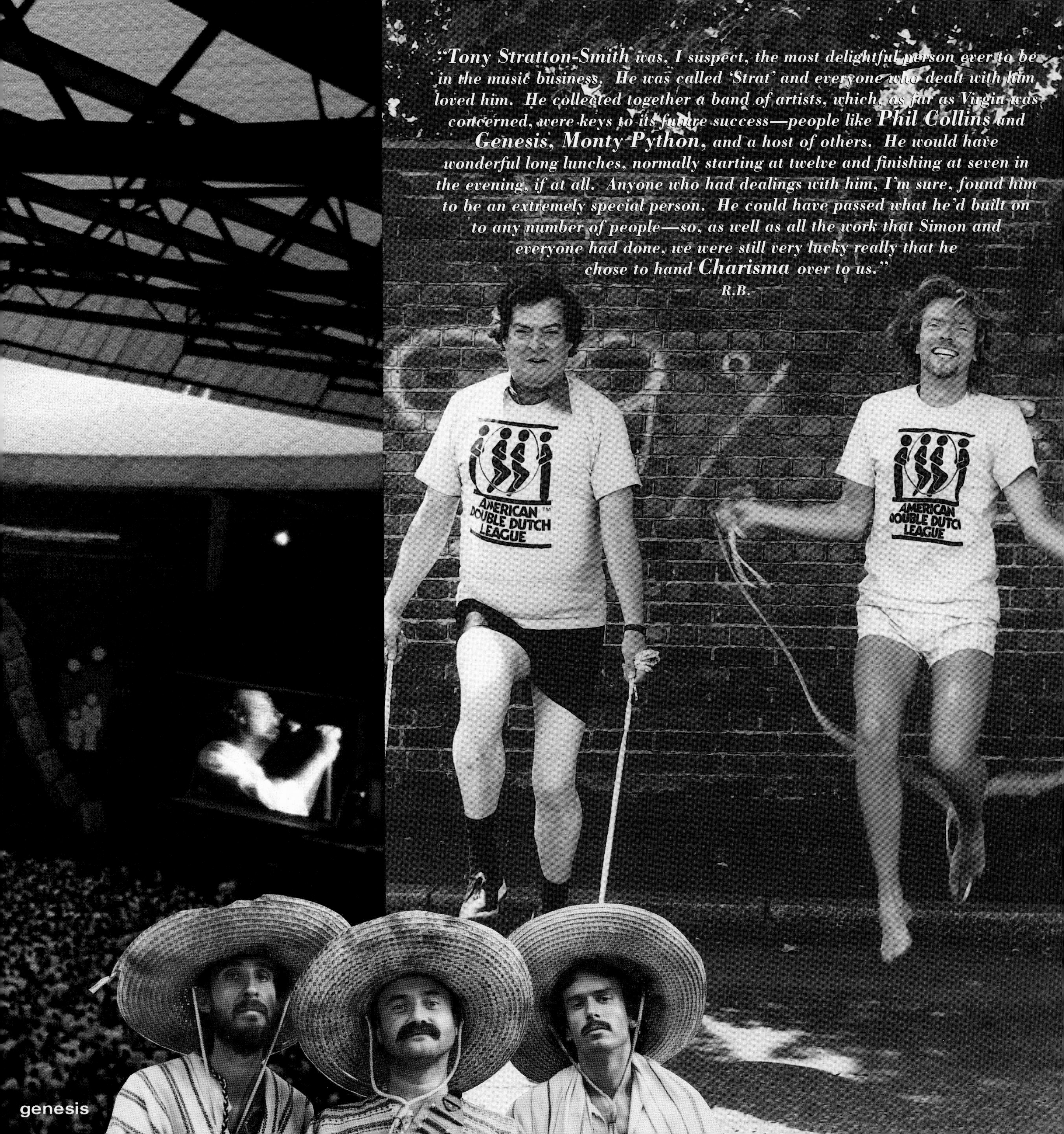

"Tony Stratton-Smith was, I suspect, the most delightful person ever to be in the music business. He was called 'Strat' and everyone who dealt with him loved him. He collected together a band of artists, which, as far as Virgin was concerned, were keys to its future success—people like **Phil Collins** *and* **Genesis, Monty Python,** *and a host of others. He would have wonderful long lunches, normally starting at twelve and finishing at seven in the evening, if at all. Anyone who had dealings with him, I'm sure, found him to be an extremely special person. He could have passed what he'd built on to any number of people—so, as well as all the work that Simon and everyone had done, we were still very lucky really that he chose to hand* **Charisma** *over to us."*

R.B.

"Music is a universal language, it draws people together and proves, as well as anything, the stupidity of racism. It's always wonderful to see the ways in which we can work together, and when the exchanges catch light, there's nothing more powerful."

Peter Gabriel

An alumnus of the ultra-exclusive Charterhouse School, young Gabriel, was, I have reason to believe, very much like the character Sebastian Marchbanks in *Brideshead Revisited.* He and two of his school chums, Mike Rutherford and Tony Banks, of similar stamp and kidney, took it upon themselves, for reasons not altogether clear, to found a "halfway decent rock ensemble" which they called **Genesis** – obviously derivative but nonetheless quite a smash.

It was a privilege I'm not likely to forget in a hurry, to have been present when Pete Gabe recalled the rather heated discussion he had with his two fine friends (right toffs they were, in my view, Ed.) about the hiring of Phil Collins to be their drummer. "They were dead against Phil from the outset," he explained. "'Who's going to wash him?'" they said. **"'We might do better to train a chimp.'"** All just bloody vicious rubbish they said against Phil. 'Look, he's part of our statement!' I said. It was as if these two had forgotten we were making a philosophic statement, you know, like Hegel or an existentialist thing. I couldn't believe it. I flashed on it, though, where they were at, where they were coming from. Class City! 'Look,' I repeated, trying to be as gentle as I could, 'I feel obliged to refer you to the counsel of one of our contemporaries, a certain squire, K. Richards.' ('He of open-fret-tuning-thing fame,' was how I put it.) His immortal words were: 'Class is not really much of a problem — I mean, not like trying to score for an oil-burner on a rainy day, if you grasp my innuendo.' They finally came around – *noblesse oblige* I suppose it was, since one of them ('Bambi John' we called him) was a direct descendant of Mary Queen of Scots."

Genesis

general public

"The first time I joined a group I was quite proud to be in a pop group. People would ask, 'What do you do?' and I'd say, 'I'm in a Pop Group.' And now you wonder if you should feel a bit embarrassed, like you're some sort of mannequin poncing about."

DAVE WAKELING, GENERAL PUBLIC

QUESTIONAIRE FOR HOT PRESS

1. First record bought and why "BLACK NIGHT" DEEP PURPLE COS ITS A GOOD RECORD

2. Favourite movie and why CHILDREN OF THE DAMNED COS IT FREAKED ME OUT WHEN I WAS A KID.

3. Song you most hate "I LOVE FISH" JOE DOLCI

4. Worst habit SMOKING

5. Who you would most like to meet and why ME TO SEE WHAT AM LIKE.

6. Favourite TV show and why DONT WATCH TELLY

7. Favourite item of clothing MY GIRLFRIENDS DENIM SHIRT

8. Biggest thrill PLAYING LIVE. SMOKING.

9. Pet hate PEOPLE ESPECIALLY IN THE MORNING

10. Favourite joke CULLY (OUR ROADIE)

it bites

It could be Bowie, could be Ray Davies, could be Sinatra, could be Nicki Lauda, could be anybody...but Marc's retirement was the best. Emotional and adamant, Marc informed the world he would have no more to do with making records...his new single will be out in a couple of weeks.

M.M. 8.86

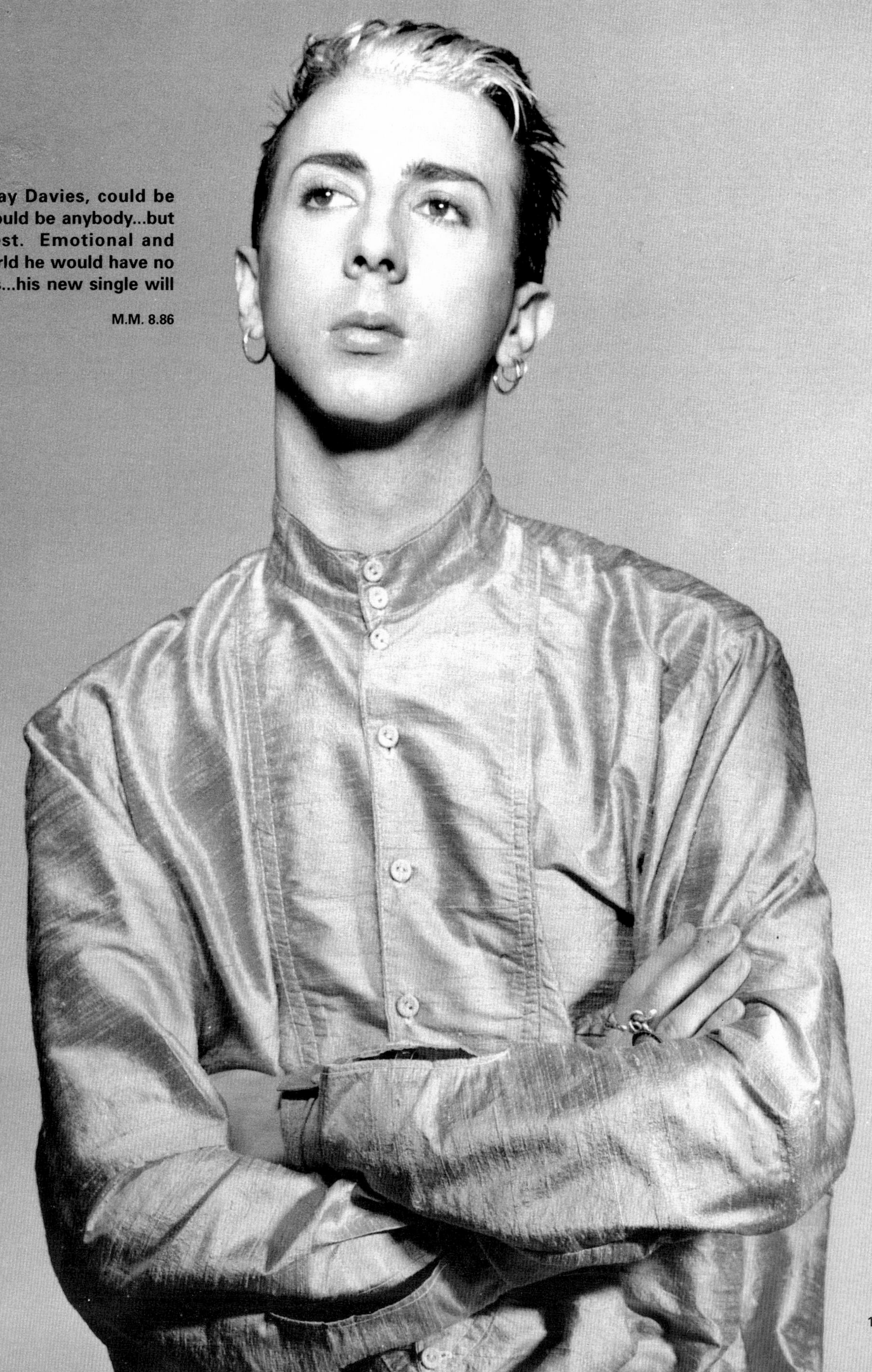

"Although I love everything I do, the problem with being a singer is that you've to get up at the crack of dawn, as often as not. And I'm quite keen to look pretty good when I'm in public, but when you've to be up early – well, any time before midday, it can sometimes be impossible. Mornings are the worst for me – I look awful, and my eyes seem to hang down to my mouth. I only feel I've come to life after I've drunk about four cups of tea. Even then, I wouldn't advise anyone to come near me for a couple of hours.

"Oh, I nearly forgot...no-one should see me last thing at night either, because, if anything, I'm worse then than I am in the morning – half a ton of face cream on – I'm like something out of the Addams Family!"

MARC ALMOND

"Another time I dumped a carrier bag of pigs' livers and maggots onto the front desk of one of the weekly papers for questioning whether or not I was for real. When they printed it, they said I'd chucked up my guts in their office! I got months of mileage out of that one."

JAZ COLEMAN, KILLING JOKE

"Gaye Bykers were great
but they didn't sell any records!"
S.D.
The fabulous Gaye Bykers on Acid have few
sacred cows and a fairly flexible agenda.

LIFE OF A POP IDLE

Why has "Always Look on the Bright Side of Life" been re-released?
It's not been released.
It's just on parole for good behaviour.

How do you view the prospect of being a pop star?
I'm looking forward to all the drugs, sex and arrests.

Do you relish the prospect of beating Cliff to the Christmas Number One slot?
Cliff who?

What do you remember about the writing of the song?
I remember nothing thanks to Halcion.

Did you resist the changing of "shit" to "spit"?
It's "shit" on the record, "spit" for broadcasting. It seems pretty silly you can't say a word for an activity everybody does.

Is there a special significance to the song?
It was sung at Graham's memorial because he loved the song.
It was sung on HMS Sheffield during the Falklands campaign when they were hit by an Exocet.
It was sung by the RAF in the Gulf.
It's sung by Manchester United fans – you figure it out.

Do you think there's a Python renaissance going on? Why?
Because it's been 500 years since the last Renaissance.

Are you a football fan? Who do you support?
A wife and two kids.

Who gets your tickets for the opera?
Jonathan Miller.

How's Hollywood?
Getting better thanks, but still not really well.

Do you see your future tied up in US TV sitcoms?
Please God no.

What vehicles do you own?
A seven-year-old Citroen.
And a pram.

What is your most-used phrase?
I'm sorry.

What is your favorite song of all time?
Tough! Too tough!
At least 100...

Do you own a parrot?
Only a dead one.

What did you think of Simon Mayo when you met him?
Who wants to know?

How are the royalties for the songs divided?
95% Virgin.
5% George Harrison.

What are you doing at the moment/ future projects?
Producing and writing a film for Prominent Features called *Hers and Graces.*

KOBAL

Eric Idle as he appears in *Monty Python's The Meaning of Life*

'I find it absolutely unbelievable that Genesis are so unhip. I listen to our music and it sounds fucking brilliant. I can't believe we're not more fashionable."

Phil Collins

(*Not* – Repeat *not* – Acceptable! Ed.)

What manner of gabfest?!?...is the Bouncing Busker about?!?

R.B. "I find it difficult to believe that you would agree to incorporate so completely a new client called Madness without any prior consultation whatsoever!"

S.D. "Well, I thought we'd been through this before when you objected to the name Rolling Stones."

R.B. "That is simply not true, and you know it! I merely expressed a passing curiosity in why they did choose that name – after all, it's not a phrase completely devoid of pejorative inference. Consider the implication of Dylan's lyrics 'How does it feel to be on your own, like a rolling stone, like a complete unknown.' "

S.D. "I've never heard such bloody rubbish! The most casual observer is surely aware that they were referencing the Muddy Waters allusion and certainly not one Robert 'Bob' Dylan."

R.B. "If indeed that is his name." (Correct. Real name Robert Allen Zimmerman, b. May 24th, Duluth, Minnesota. Ed.)

madness

Following the success of the jock group **Gaye Bykers on Acid,** Virgin decided to go for a repeat performance, this time with an assortment of lorry drivers as an all-femme group (supposedly all-femme, Ed.), **Lesbian Dopeheads on Mopeds,** and under astute guidance, the group was soon chart-wise bound. Some critics said they had "real musical talent," but in the eyes of most, they remained primarily a **novelty group.** (As they do to this day, in my humble opinion. Ed.)

"She had quite a big success for Virgin America – but they were still losing money – and suddenly, and seemingly quite miraculously, she took off. I went out to America with Kenny for a big crisis meeting with Jordan and Jeff (top American execs, Ed.) worried about the amount of money they were spending; we were to go through their artists' roster with them. One of the artists they were getting ready to drop was Paula Abdul; they were spending all this money on her and it hadn't really happened. It's unbelievable, but at lunchtime we sat in on a marketing meeting where they were arguing about this remix of her single, and on that same day the thing suddenly started to turn around, orders started to pile in, and the record took off like a rocket – played a major role in establishing Virgin America – but it was that close! Another week and they might have got rid of her."

S.D.

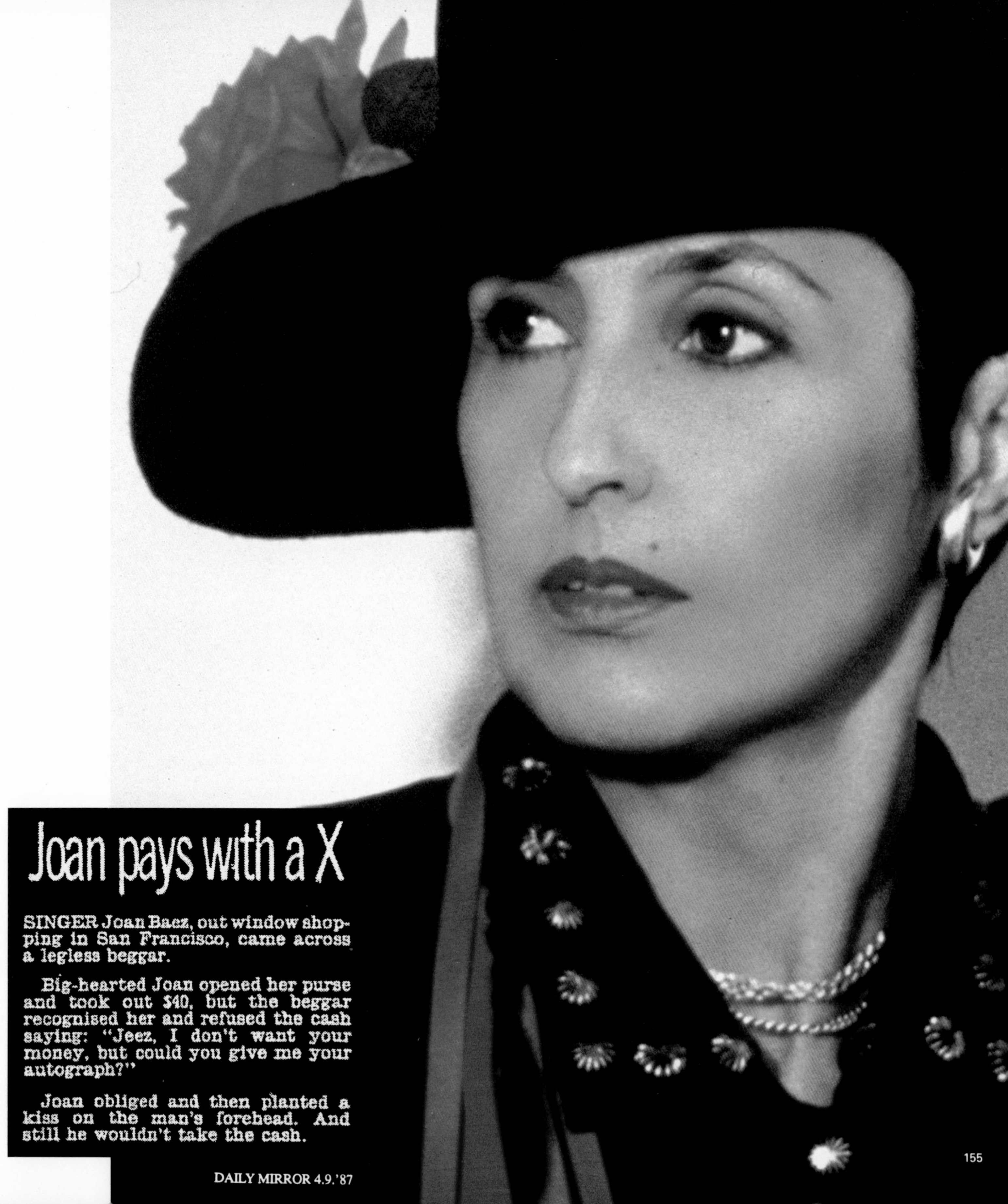

Joan pays with a X

SINGER Joan Baez, out window shopping in San Francisco, came across a legless beggar.

Big-hearted Joan opened her purse and took out $40, but the beggar recognised her and refused the cash saying: "Jeez, I don't want your money, but could you give me your autograph?"

Joan obliged and then planted a kiss on the man's forehead. And still he wouldn't take the cash.

DAILY MIRROR 4.9.'87

Johnny Hates Jazz rehearsing for their hit single "Shattered Dreams."

T'Pau, having taken their name from a "Star Trek" character, promptly proceeded to reach Number Four in the U.S. of A. and in '87 hit the ever-lucky Number One spot in the U.K. with "China in Your Hand."

LOUD and dirty deviant music!
You like it?
You want more? what about the 'Blood Uncles' then? They have aggression, menace and mayhem — and they're in 'Kilmarnock' this weekend.
M.M. 8.87

Peter Gabriel, Youssou N'Dour, and friends deliver for real.

KX88

mahlathin

nusrat fateh ali kahn

thomas mapfumo

dudu pukwana

"A lot more people have hear 'Higher Love' than 'Gimme Som Lovin.' Or, often people hear 'Gimme Some Lovin' and don' know it's me. That happens a lo They say, 'Why are you coverin that Blues Brothers song?' I wa working for quite some tim with Tom (Lord Alge, who co engineered Winwood's 198 smash *Back in the High Life* an co-produced the album *Roll wi It*) and something came up an we talked about 'I'm a Man,' an Tom said, 'You don't mean "I'm Man, yes I am..."' I said, 'Yeah He said 'You wrote that?' I sai 'Yeah.' You know, he just reall didn't know.

"Ray Charles wa my ultimate hero

still is. I copied everything h did. I even met him briefly: sweet southern man who call everyone 'sir.' Since being i Nashville, I have learnt a lo about those songs which were s influential to me as a fifteen-yea old. I've filled in all the back ground and even met many of th people who played on them Like, did you know when Arthu Alexander made 'You Bette Move On,' he was a bell-hop in downtown hotel? The whole c Spencer Davis was based o those sorts of records."

STEVE WINWOO

"You take about four or five of those rattlesnakes, dry 'em out, and put them inside your hollow box guitar. Lightnin' Hopkins taught me that trick. He was my idol, man. That was my beginning – him and John Lee Hooker. I love the records I'm working on now too – the songs have this great R&B feel, which is something I've always loved."

ALBERT COLLINS

Bryan Ferry with an interpretation of *The Death of Marat*

"The Tams were great! 'My Baby Sure Can Shag,' I think, was the follow-up. The one before that was 'There Ain't Nothing Like Shaggin'.' They even made a film called *Shag...*" S.D. Jenny (Simon's extremely personable assistant, Ed.): "We had T-shirts printed up with everything we could think of about shagging all over them! It was brilliant."

Barry: "I've got what it takes. Sexual inadequacy."

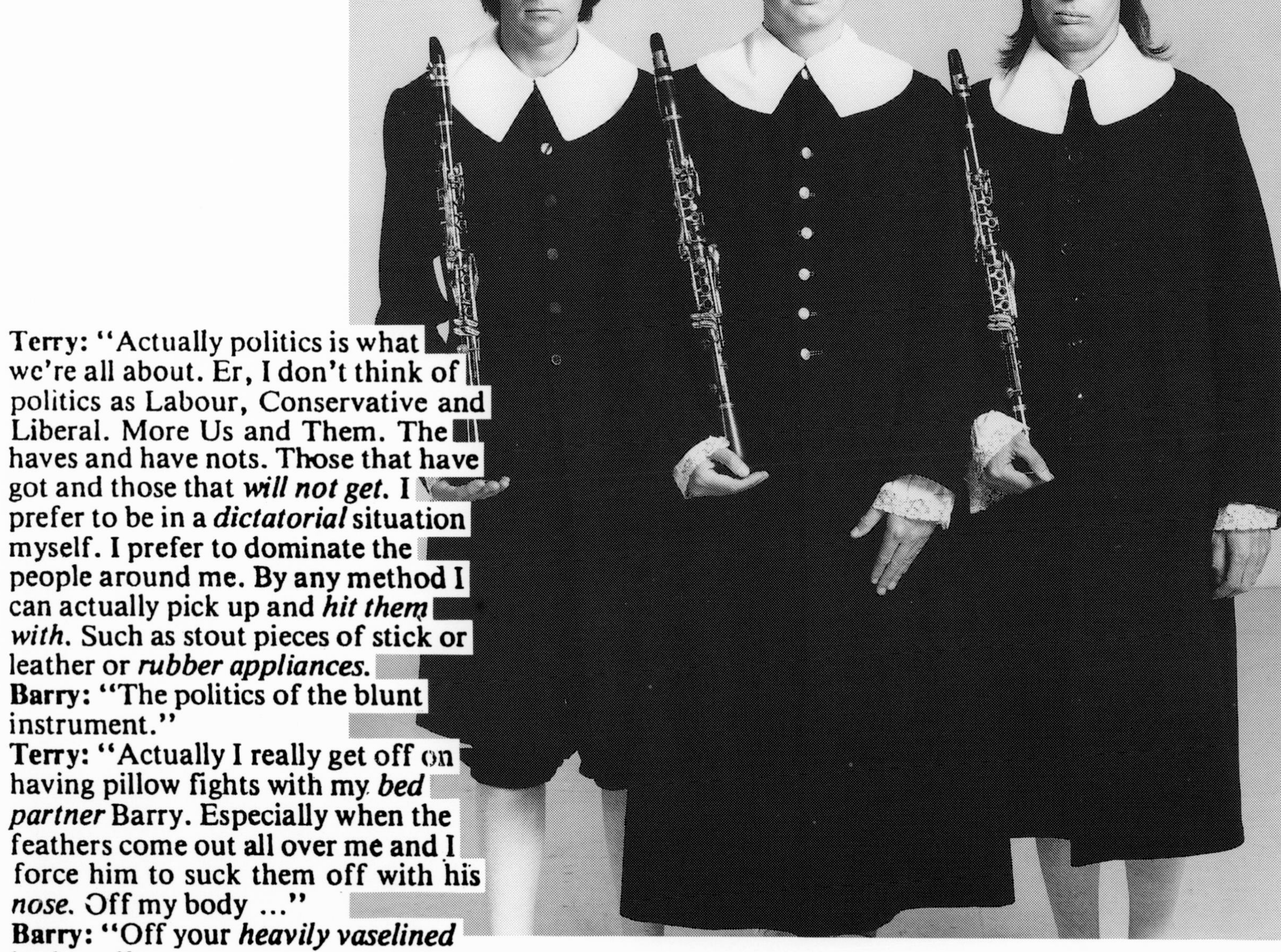

Terry: "Actually politics is what we're all about. Er, I don't think of politics as Labour, Conservative and Liberal. More Us and Them. The haves and have nots. Those that have got and those that *will not get*. I prefer to be in a *dictatorial* situation myself. I prefer to dominate the people around me. By any method I can actually pick up and *hit them with*. Such as stout pieces of stick or leather or *rubber appliances*.
Barry: "The politics of the blunt instrument."
Terry: "Actually I really get off on having pillow fights with my *bed partner* Barry. Especially when the feathers come out all over me and I force him to suck them off with his *nose*. Off my body ..."
Barry: "Off your *heavily vaselined* body ..."
Terry: "And rub *lard* into my chest And *fry eggs* on it. My *hot* body."

"I can't go in a mini-cab. I'm a cult."

GARY GLITTER

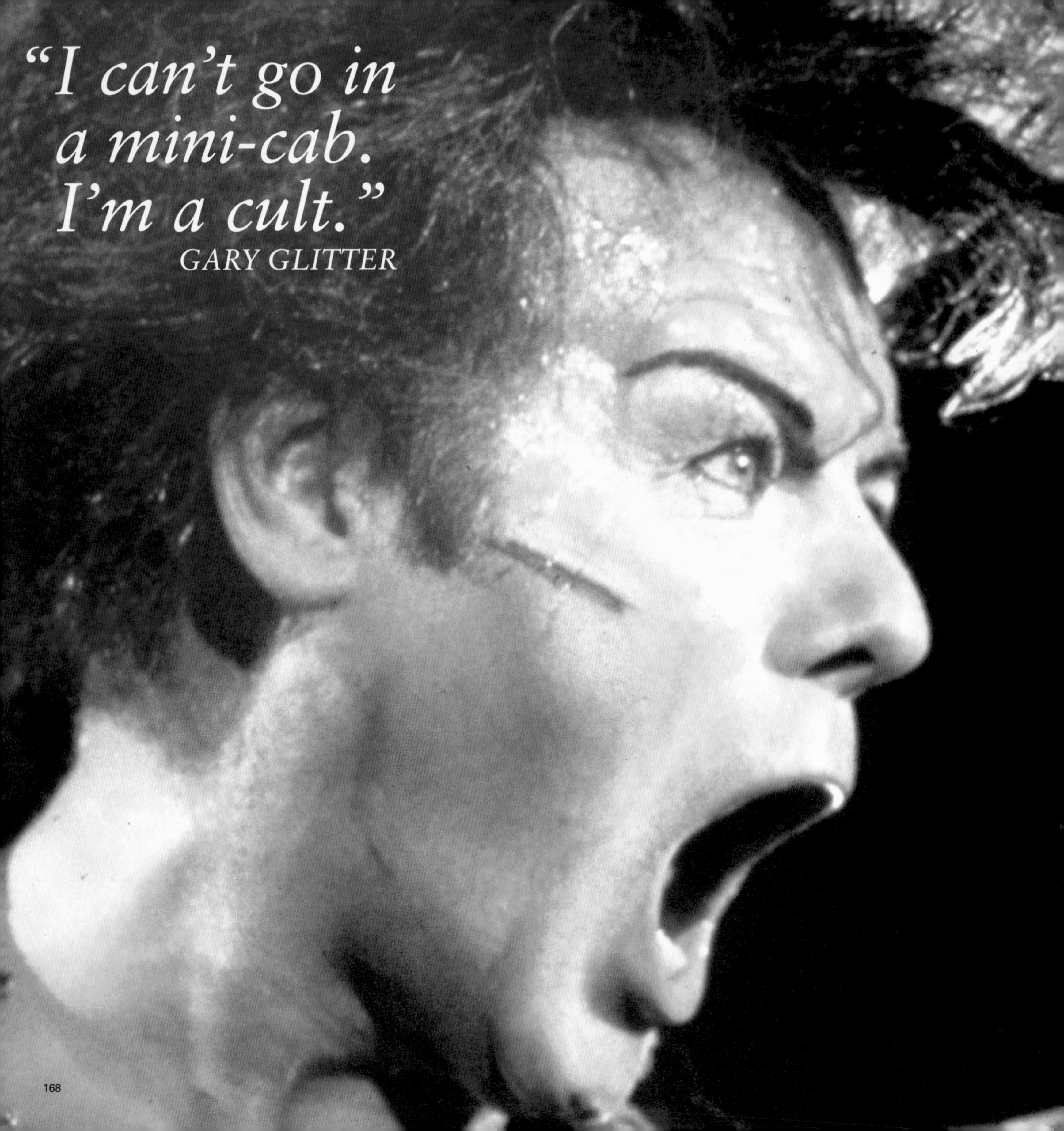

S. D.: "There was no artist who had ever been to the record company's offices that had caused such a stir – some people went home to change – to get a different outfit."

Jenny: "People hanging off the banisters – I was having palpitations, I mean, I just nearly died."

S. D.: "Plus he made a good record – we very nearly got it away, that single."

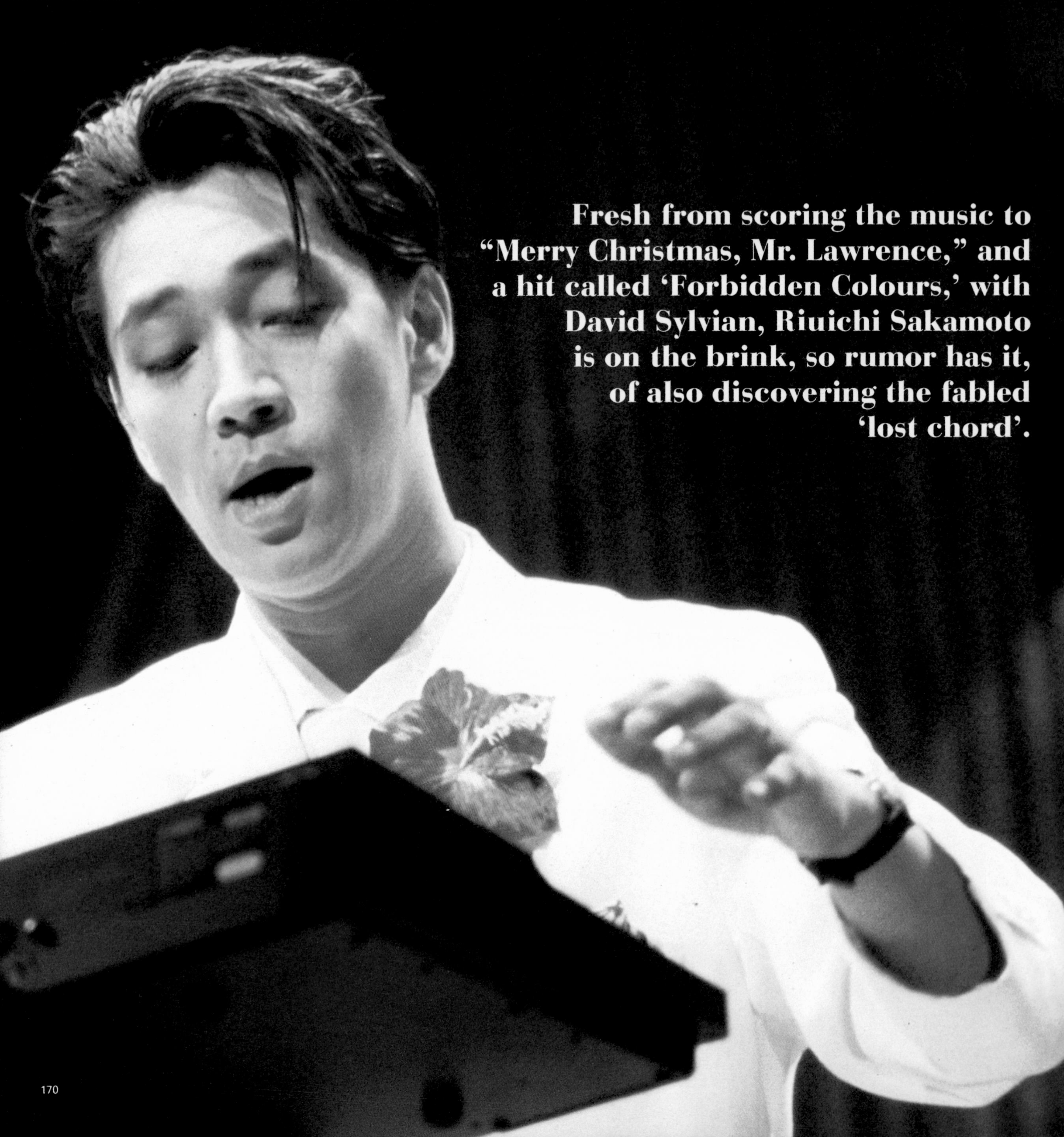

Fresh from scoring the music to "Merry Christmas, Mr. Lawrence," and a hit called 'Forbidden Colours,' with David Sylvian, Riuichi Sakamoto is on the brink, so rumor has it, of also discovering the fabled 'lost chord'.

Looking for a friend

Gregory Kane from Hue and Cry has been telling me how much he hated living in America when they were recording their album *Remote*. "I lived in New York for four months and it wasn't until the last week that I actually made a friend. It's very difficult in New York because unless you can do them a favour, people really don't want to know you." Somewhat different to things back home where brother Patrick got the inspiration for their new single "Looking for Linda" from a woman he met on a train. "She was running away from her husband, and she told me her whole story in fifteen minutes between train stops!"

YORKSHIRE EVENING POST 21.1.89

R.B., with his vast PR savvy, had a qualm or two about this particular presentation of their new group That Petrol Emotion, and he was not long in expressing as much to Simon Draper. "In this representation," he said, "they have literally **targeted themselves!** Has there ever been a more flagrant Freudian slip in the history of psychoanalysis? Literally issuing a cry for help against suicide." "What bloody rubbish!" replied the Mave rather sharply. "They are all getting more ass than a toilet seat! Young men don't commit suicide in situations like that!" "I cannot believe that you said that," said R.B., "simply cannot buh-lieve it! It actually makes me think that you are urgently in need of psychoanalytic help yourself. I'm sorry, but it's true!" This set the Mave fairly hopping. "Will you get on with your rubbish!" he exclaimed. "And your *CRACKPOT GIBBERISH!*"

Julian Lennon, warts and all, has taken on the robes of his father with great aplomb and more than enough talent to have made his parents proud.

Pandora's Box, mysterious and multi-talented, though not perhaps altogether prudent to fling open with complete abandon.

"People keep on cheering for **encores**, but we run out of songs to play. That never happens to other groups. Maybe we should **write some more.**"

P.J.

At the instigation of Big Dick and the Mave (and over the strenuous objections of K.B., who kept shouting, "Bad form! Shame!" etc.), Roy Orbison tries to woo young Billy Idol to the Virgin label. (Their audacious efforts were to nil advantage. Ed.)

"I've been writing with all kinds of people – I'll go to Will Jennings' house to write, then to Steve Croppers', then Steve Jones of the Sex Pistols, or T-Bone Burnett. It sounds like I'm doing a lot, maybe, for this stage of my career, but by doing that I'm a better person, I sleep better, I'm a better father and husband. It's dawned on me that it's not the goals you set – the next Grammy or the million-seller – but the doing of the things, and the people you meet along the way."

ROY ORBISON

The lovely

Belinda Carlisle strolls by the light of her own lagoon.

"**Personally,** I think that the ideal **record company should be run by people between the ages of seventeen and twenty-five** who are single, hungry, willing to go out clubbing every night, you know, be in touch with the musicians, be in touch with what's going on. The year or two before we sold, we were floundering a little bit – we weren't breaking new acts, and I just think we didn't have our ears to the ground as much as we should have done.

"I'd already really moved away from the record company a good few years to '92, but as long as Simon was completely committed, I was very happy for him to continue building Virgin. I think a combination of factors took place in '92. The airline suffered a major attack from British Airways in the form of their whole dirty tricks campaign which went on systematically for about eighteen months. So that although I never would have thought of selling before, as an insurance policy against the banks becoming too worried, I began to listen to what other record companies had to say.

"At the same time, Simon had become less involved in the record company than he'd previously been and was definitely interested in moving into other areas. Then the third factor was that Ken Berry was willing to look after Virgin Records, stay with it one hundred and ten percent, make sure that it remained an independent company within the EMI umbrella, and I think has done a magnificent job in accomplishing that.

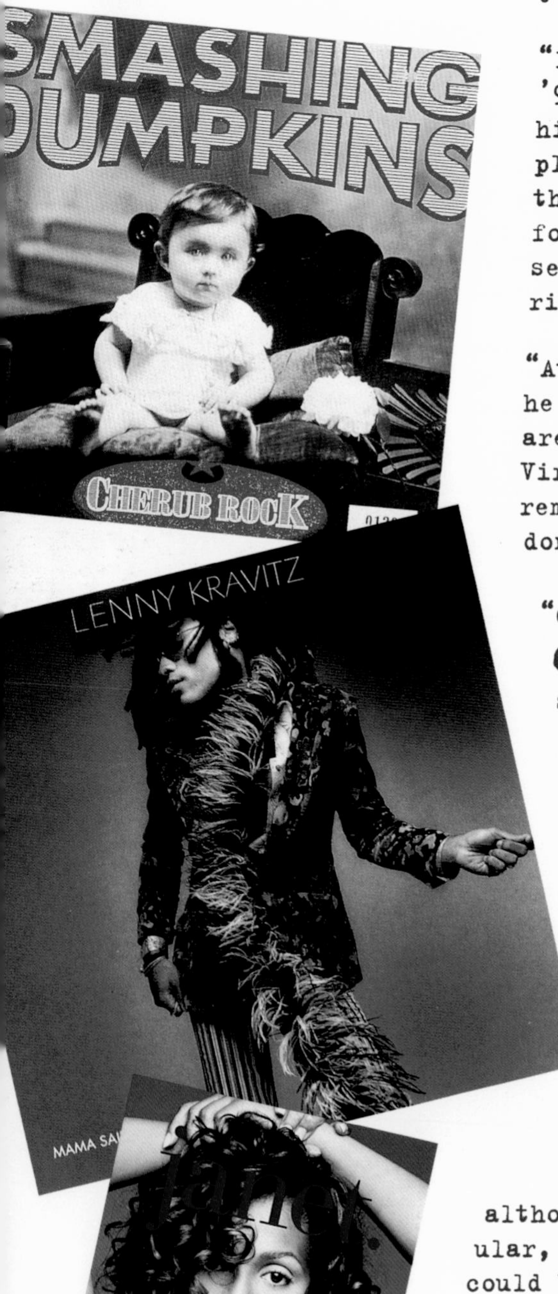

"Obviously, in a sense, **it was very sad on the day of the sale,** and I found it extremely difficult talking to the staff the day it happened. But in another sense it was as if the company had come of age. One can't keep everything forever in life, and the resources we got from the sale has enabled us to move on, expand the airline, start up new businesses, hopefully get permission to run the lottery and other things.

"Also I do believe that Virgin Records is in some ways stronger today than it was under our ownership in '92. I mean, Ken has done what we perhaps should have done. He took tough decisions, particularly in tidying up the roster, which we hadn't got the strength to do, and he's got an extremely impressive company now.

"The last two signings we made were Janet Jackson and the Rolling Stones. I knew that there was a possibility that we would sell, but I was still rather hoping that the label would continue with us. So although I didn't view it as such at the time, I suppose the Stones in particular, as our last signing and after twenty years of my trying to sign them, could be looked upon as a kind of final swan song." R.B.

'After we'd privatized, there was definitely no decision to sell the music company. We had plans to continue to build it up under independent-ownership wealth, but we all had different things going on in our lives, particularly by '92. Richard's real interest was in the airline, had been pretty much since the time it was founded – he loved it. He'd become less actively concerned about actually running a music company and obviously, by selling it, he generated a very significant amount of money to enable him to consolidate his success. Simon, I think, had his own perspective on it. I don't think he was as passionately interested in the music at that particular point as he had been in prior years, but I suppose if the right price hadn't been around, it wouldn't have been sold and we would still be an independent company, owned privately as opposed to by Thorn-EMI. As far as I am concerned, however, I've enjoyed every minute of the years with Virgin. I love the people that make it up, I love working with artists and their managers, it's what I do. I love doing it, and for me to actually stop being part of Virgin would be virtually unthinkable.

"I remember back in 1974 walking down Portobello Road and hearing someone in their flat playing *Tubular Bells*. I heard it coming out of the window and for the first time it dawned on me, 'Good heavens, it's successful!' That's what it's all about. That music's not just about me playing it at home or people playing it at the office, but about people actually buying it, taking it home, listening, and truly liking it, so it's shared. **That's great.**

"You have enormous expectations and hopes for the success of all kinds of records which are in the making, and sometimes you're right and sometimes you're wrong as to commercial success, and obviously you still like them whichever way it goes. But you always have something new going on – and that's the best part, really – when everyone's really excited by new bands on the label yet to release their first record and you can't wait for them to take off. Or when an artist's been successful with you before and they're back in the studio making another record and it feels really great and you're looking forward to it so much! These are all the positive things that go on every year, and it just doesn't stop. That's what motivates us, I think, to just have that constant stream of quality music coming through."

K.B.

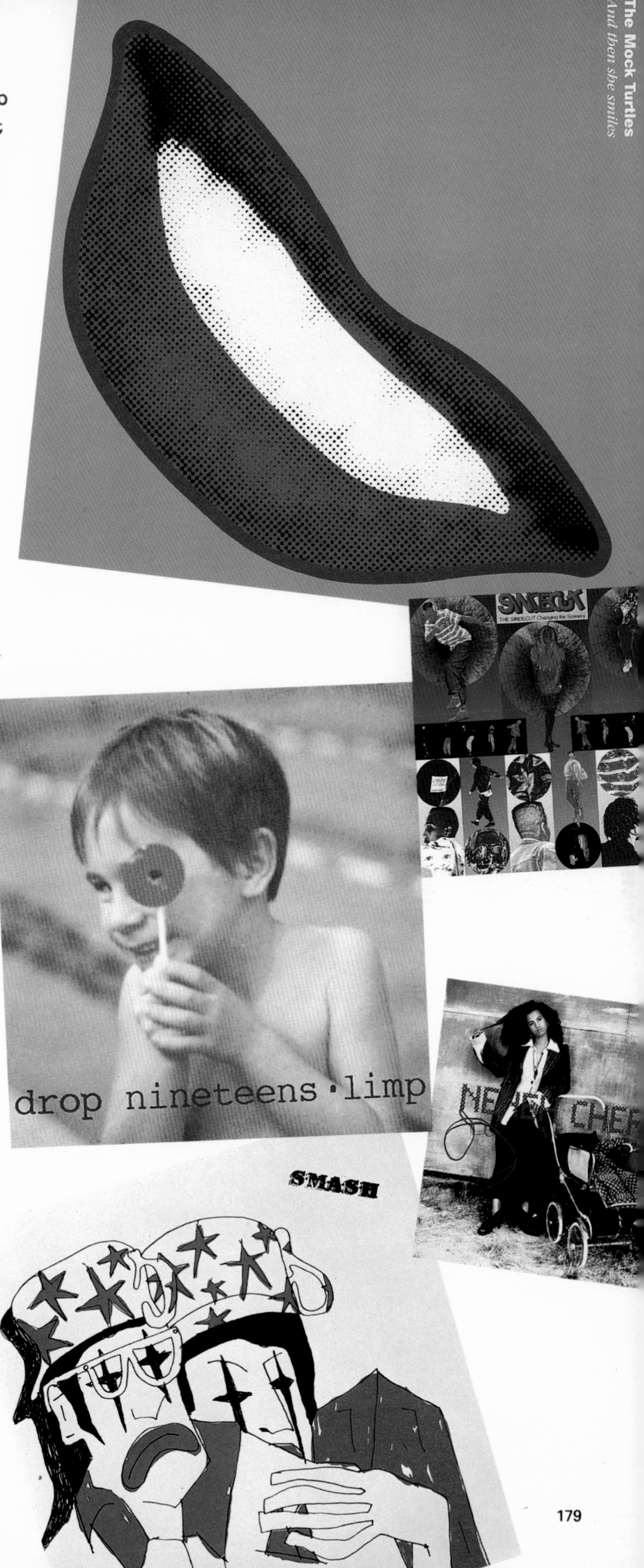

The faces of dance and rap are as diverse as the lyrics and moves of the music itself.

massive attack

definition of sound

"We're not born out of the **musician** thing, we're born out of the DJ thing."

3-D, MASSIVE ATTACK

redhead kingpin

sindecut

The happy faces of **Ziggy** (son o' Bob) **Marley** and his **Melody Makers** as their Land Rover is poised before plunging into the **Jamaican bush** en route for more *tip-top* jamming...

... While ten thousand miles to the west,

the veteran blues guitarist Terry Evans kicks back in the cool of the **Memphis** evening.

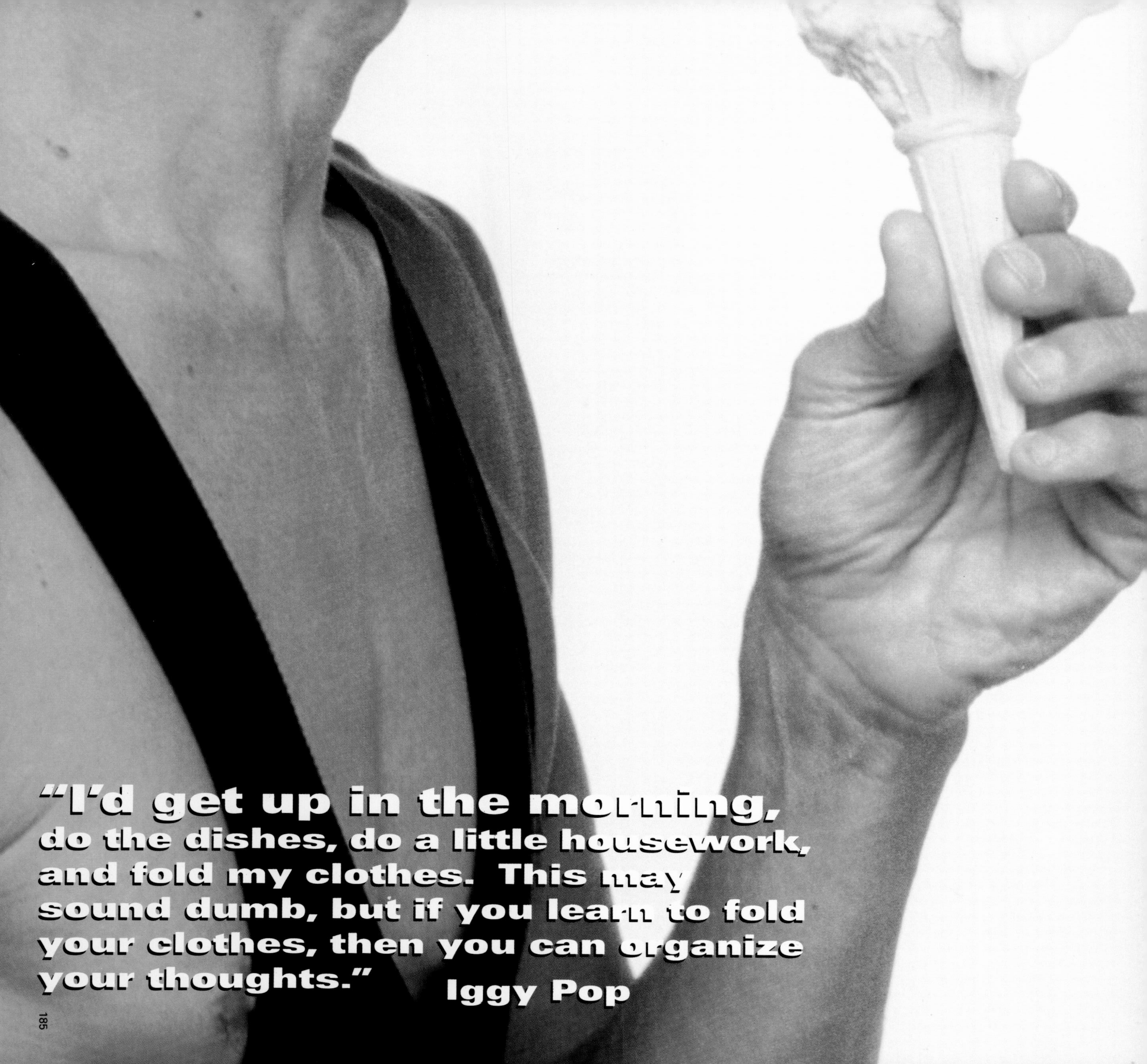

"I'd get up in the morning, do the dishes, do a little housework, and fold my clothes. This may sound dumb, but if you learn to fold your clothes, then you can organize your thoughts."

Iggy Pop

Meat Loaf (a.k.a. Marvin Lee Aday) first distinguished himself as Eddie the Frozen Rocker in *The Rocky Horror Picture Show.* He met Jim Steinman, the so-called sci-fi prancer, while working with "The National Lampoon Road Show," and the duo composed a grandiose rock opera entitled *Bat Out of Hell.* After this, Meat Loaf's career dipped slightly until Virgin performed what they call their "Lazarus Number" on him and not only put him and Jim Steinman back in the studio cutting tracks together again, but guided his meteoric return to lucky Number One status

iggy pop

A.K.A. John Jack Rotten

trying to look pleasant for a change as he dreams of the days when he used to trash cathedrals and orphanages with his friend Sidney Vish.

The Smashing Pumpkins soak up a few rays. *(Building a tan for a forthcoming performance, touch wood. Ed.)*

"That was an experience – brilliant. It was the first time I'd been to Jamaica, too. Everybody's musical in mind out there. Recording there is best for vibes and comfort, but equipment-wise, there's a lot more equipment in England. You don't get the tape breaking down, or power cuts for four hours happening halfway through the song."
MAXI PRIEST

"Am I all ready to be a role model?
Yes, I am. From an early age, when I'd wised up to current affairs and the fact that black youths were considered newsworthy only in a negative sense, I knew there was a need not just for me, but people like me. And the fact that I've done something, that I'm getting recognition from business levels or sound systems or whatever, shows that it can be done. Your wildest dreams can become reality if you put your mind to it, you stick to what you believe in."
JAZZIE B.

"You go to
the clubs, you rave,
you hear the new music,
see the new dances,
see the fashions, you
can meet, socialize, and
most important of all,
you can express yourself."
– Jazzie B. of Soul II Soul making tracks with James Brown

“Signing Janet was symbolic in some ways. First of all, she was at the time already one of the top worldwide recording artists. She was most particularly incredibly successful in America, so to agree to sign with Virgin was a gesture of confidence in our ability to deliver success in her own domestic market. The fact that we were in a position to compete with the other majors to sign Janet was a bit like a coming of age.”

K. B.

"During the ***L.A. riot*** *Channel 11 (L.A. TV station) comes running up to my house. They get me in front of the camera and say,* ***'Tell 'em to stop! You're on.'*** *I'm thinkin', Tell 'em to stop!? And I just spilled from my heart.*

*"I said, 'I hate to say I told you it was going to happen, but anybody who's surprised by this...**it's your fault**, and I don't like looking at this, this is my neighborhood. But I can't honestly say that if I didn't have this money in my pocket, I wouldn't be out there, 'cause I'm really pissed.' They're saying, 'Get this guy off the air! What is he doin'?' They fired the guy that got me down there."*

ICE-T

"From my point of view, during the L.A. riots I was here in Sweden and

it was like Judgment Day.

"Unfortunately, there's gonna be a lot of bloodshed because it's not the kinda thing that's going to go down in a peaceful way. The American government ain't got no fucking sympathy and neither has the general American public.

"I didn't write a song about it, but if I'm asked to speak about it, I'll say what I think."

NENEH CHERRY

The production services of husband Cameron McVey on *Raw Like Sushi* brought Neneh some rather fickle criticism which she's quick to dismiss, insisting that McVey and Johnny Dollar were always part of a team. "Quite often groups fall apart when individuals think it's just them and everyone goes off on their little ego trips, whereas in fact what makes music interesting is the chemistry between people.

"A lot of the flavours and emotions I had on the first album haven't gone. When you go away from something, that's when you come to terms with things in your subconscious. When we started making this next record, there was a sort of tenderness to it that was completely new to us. We all felt pretty relaxed, and it all came together. I found that with my singing voice I was battling against things, but here I could get away from whatever it was that I was having the problem with, so when I came back to sing, I was more likely to do it right."

NENEH CHERRY

"John Lee – seventy-odd years old and he's so together there's chicks at his house, and they all play guitar, and he's the guitar teacher. I thought, This is what I need – a female rock and roll guitar school. When I get to seventy-five, if I could run something like that..."
KEITH RICHARDS

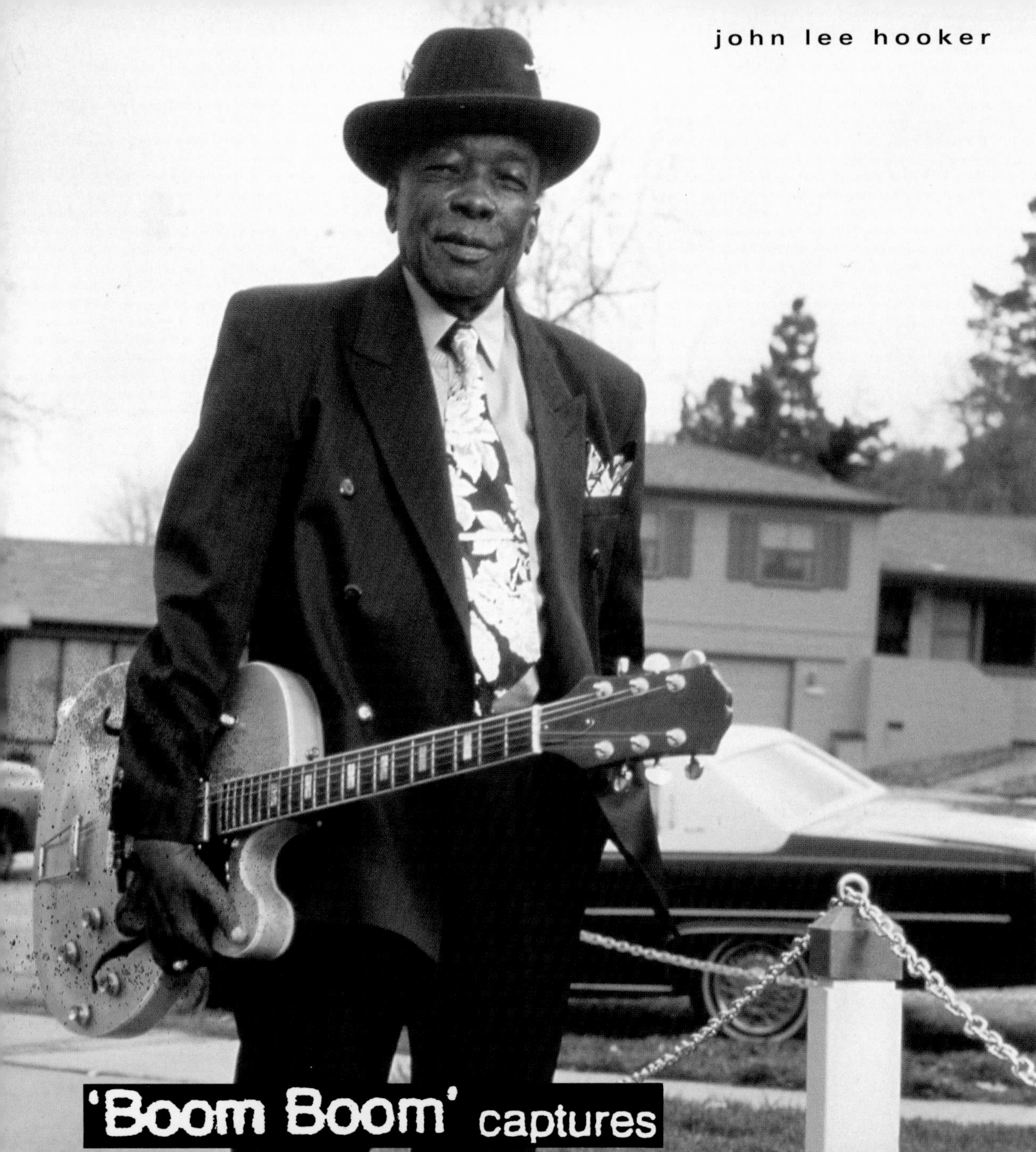

'Boom Boom' captures that moment when you walk into a bar, or some place, and go 'whoo, I'd sure like to take her home with me tonight!' Making love is the best experience there is and, no matter how old I get, that'll never change."

John Lee Hooker

'Keith Richards? Such a nice man. Don't have no ego, no ego trip at all.'

JOHN LEE HOOKER

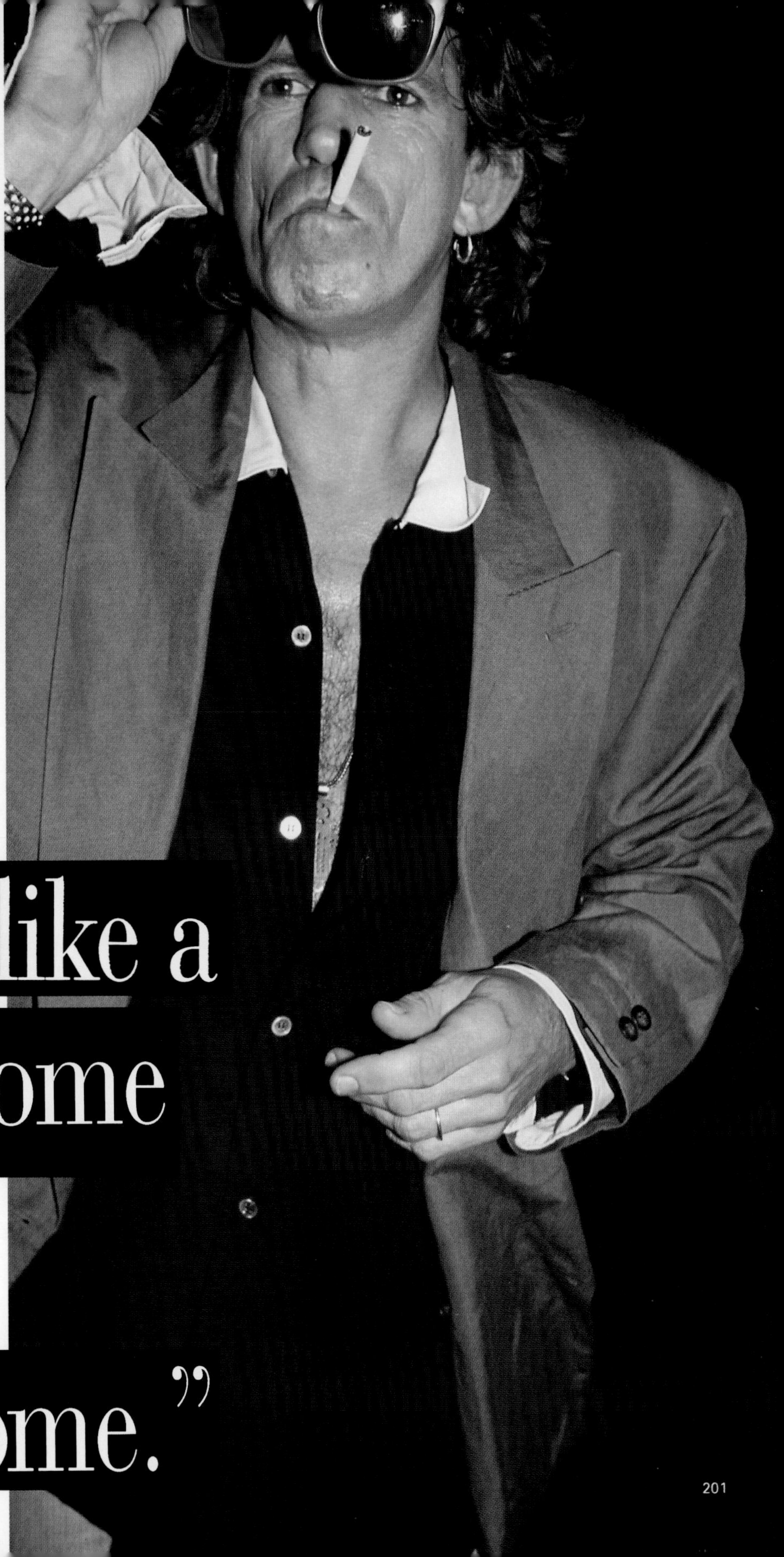

"I do like a good girl to come home to. if I have a home."

Keith Richards

"I was having a Bev Hills lunch with big Bill 'Stretch' Claxton, photographer to the stars and celebs, when he suddenly confided in me about a recent session he had just completed. 'It was down Texas way,' he said. 'I was doing some human-interest shots in a Tex-Mex whorehouse. The girls were exquisite – "Mexicale Rose," you know the type – all luscious red mouth, big brown eyes, pert knockers and derriere, and the sort of willowy limbs you immediately want wrapped around your head. I was on my second roll of Triple X Kodachrome when I heard the strumming of a guitar from a distant room and a plaintive ballad being sung in a soft nasal twang, characteristic of Texas and the great southwest. I followed the haunting chords down a dimly lit corridor until I reached the source of the lilting melody — a small room with a bed and a single yellow bulb suspended from the ceiling.

" 'An incredibly beautiful girl was lying on the bed wearing little more than her lavender lipstick. Sitting in the only chair in the room, a western guitar across his lap, was a lanky wrangler type, in jeans, boots, and a well-travelled hat. 'I hope I'm not interrupting,' I said, and ventured a couple of shots on a low-light setting. When I started tightening focus, I was surprised to see that the nipples of the girl's perfect breasts were in taut distention – 'surprised' because I had no idea that the viewfinder on this camera had such a high resolution. I was considering another tight-focus shot, on perhaps a different area of this extraordinary bod, when I suddenly realized, from the Muddy Waters/Lightnin' Hopkins blues licks which were emanating from the guitar, that this fellow could be none other than the great John Jack Winter.

"'I was about to inquire in that regard, when he leaned the guitar against the bed, sighed audibly, and walked over to the window and stared out in a pensive manner. Not wishing to intrude on his private thoughts, I took a quick shot of him in his reverie. I have always thought of it as one of my better Cartier-Bresson-type shots.'"

johnny winter

"I tried to sign the Stones for twenty years.

I was determined, I mean, I remember one night in 1974, I went to see them, and even though I didn't have the money, I offered their manager a deal which was a lot better than the one they had at the time. He was intrigued. He said, 'Look, by Monday morning I want to have on my desk a banker's guarantee for the deal you're putting up, because I don't believe it.' So I was, what, twenty-one years old then, and I spent the weekend flying around Europe, to Ariola and our other licensees, and by Monday morning I walked into his office with the banker's guarantee. All the manager did was to simply take the banker's guarantee and up the deal accordingly with whatever record company he was already dealing with. No problem. But anyway, twenty years later, it's still a blast to know that finally their record's coming out. And on Virgin." R. B.

"I went to a school in New York 'round the corner from where I grew up o MacDougal Street, called the Little Red Schoolhouse. It was multi-cultura with all colours and races. There was a music teacher there called Charit Bailey, a black woman, I guess then in her forties. She made sure that ever child in her class played a musical instrument, be it the piano or a Chines gong. This was in 1948 or '49. I'm sure she knew Leadbelly (Huddi Ledbetter), well, because he was a guy that got around. Anyway, we sang hi songs, because when I was five, six, seven years old, that's what everybody i the school did. So I became musically aware at a very early age, not througl my father (the legendary John Hammond, Sr., who discovered a host of talen from Billie Holiday to Bob Dylan and Bruce Springsteen, and produced th 1965 Sun House sessions), but through Charity Bailey. When I started listen ing to the radio, I gravitated towards the music that had that good feeling And by the time I hit my teens, I was into the blues. In 1957 a Folkway album called *The Country Blues* came out, compiled by Sam Charters, an I picked that up because it had an intriguing title. There were artists lik Leroy Carr and Scrapper Blackwell. I could see the link between th different stages of the music. These guys were playing all by them selves, and they were playing better than anything I'd ever heard. had my eye out for anything like that and by the time I was seventeen I was a fully-fledged blues fanatic

"When I was eighteen, I went to a prestigious art school in Maine, and my roommate, Leo Robinson, was black and he had a guitar on which he would play folk songs. When he wasn't around, I'd go up to the room and try to strum chords. I got right into it. That fall, I went to a college in Ohi and within a week I'd bought my first guitar from a girl for ten dollars. I just went feverishly at trying to put into music all the blues songs I heard in my head. Because I knew all the words of the songs, I could sing them. Within a year and a half, when I was nineteen, I was play- ing professionally."

JOHN HAMMOND

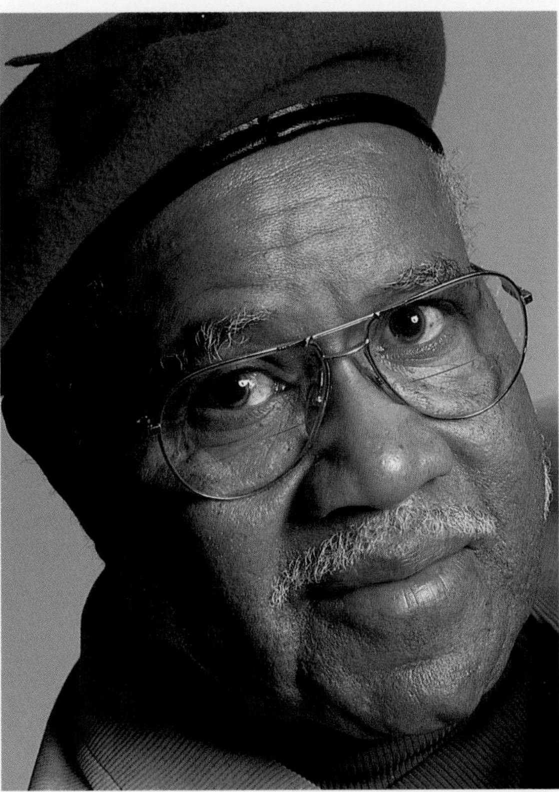

"My daddy was a farmer, but that was something I didn't care for. I said to myself that I was going to get away. I could get five dollars a night playing the blues, against three dollars a week working on the farm – but I always wanted to be on the Gospel side.

"I was already married by then with two children when we moved up-river to Chicago. At first I washed cars, then I got a job in the stockyards, and later I moved to the steel mill. And I let my guitar get away from me. My wife was having children so fast that I didn't have time to play. Then one day I was talking to a man who told me he had a guitar in a pawnshop, and he said that if I wanted to get it out of there I could have it. It was seven dollars, I think, and that's when I started playing and singing with the children. Pervis sang lead until his voice got too heavy, so I said, 'You move down to baritone and let Mavis sing the lead.' She was only about fourteen years old, but she came out there and took over. If Pervis had stayed singing lead, I'd never have known. The Lord worked that way."

ROEBUCK "POPS" STAPLES

"If you look at the cars that arrive at my rehearsals, you'll see who's getting the most money. I came on a bicycle..."

GARY MOORE

Robert Fripp (the old King Crimson, to be quite frank about it) has formed a most intriguing liaison with Japan's ever-evolving **David Sylvian**. "Stand by for some rather volatile chemistry," is how Mave Draper expressed it.

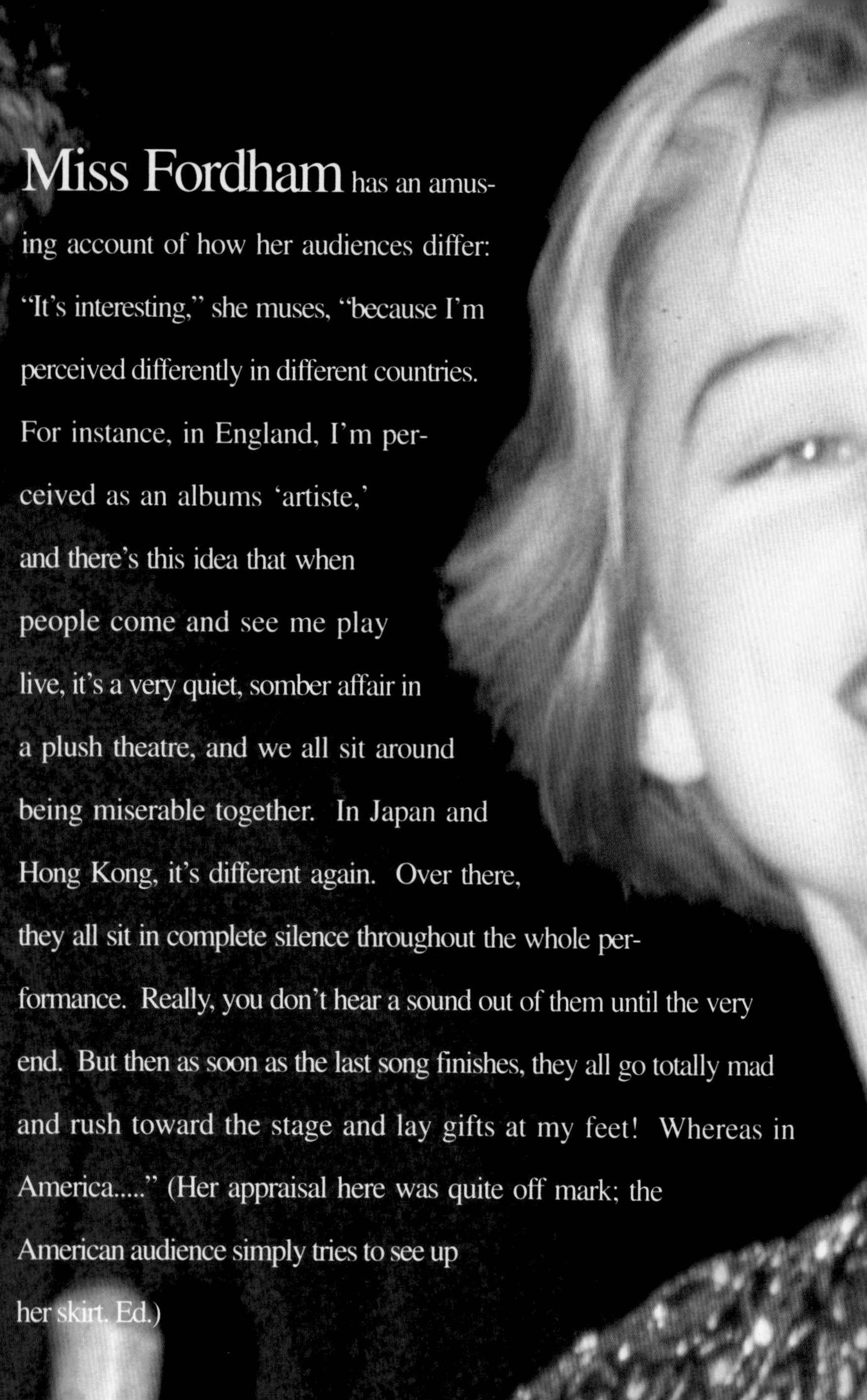

Miss Fordham has an amusing account of how her audiences differ: "It's interesting," she muses, "because I'm perceived differently in different countries. For instance, in England, I'm perceived as an albums 'artiste,' and there's this idea that when people come and see me play live, it's a very quiet, somber affair in a plush theatre, and we all sit around being miserable together. In Japan and Hong Kong, it's different again. Over there, they all sit in complete silence throughout the whole performance. Really, you don't hear a sound out of them until the very end. But then as soon as the last song finishes, they all go totally mad and rush toward the stage and lay gifts at my feet! Whereas in America....." (Her appraisal here was quite off mark; the American audience simply tries to see up her skirt. Ed.)

Perhaps the first point to appreciate about an **enigma** is that it is indeed an enigma.

The legendary **Brian Eno**, a conceptual artist of the first order, caught the eye of the avant-garde when he appeared with Ferry's Roxy Music tastefully decked out in furs and **peacock feathers.** A celebration of decadence and narcissism is said to have reached a nadir when **Brian Eno** and **David Bowie** shared a Berlin stage.

Richie Branson has shown a certain ambivalence towards the new group **Jellyfish**. "It is not a term," he explained, "which evokes great confidence in the GBP. Are you aware that the Australian jellyfish is among the world's **most venomous** and **despised creatures?** Where are these chaps from anyway?" Draper, though poised to deliver a **devastating** riposte, on this occasion at least, felt disposed to spare his beloved partner any further chagrin.

Salv of Smash
practising unsafe bass playing.

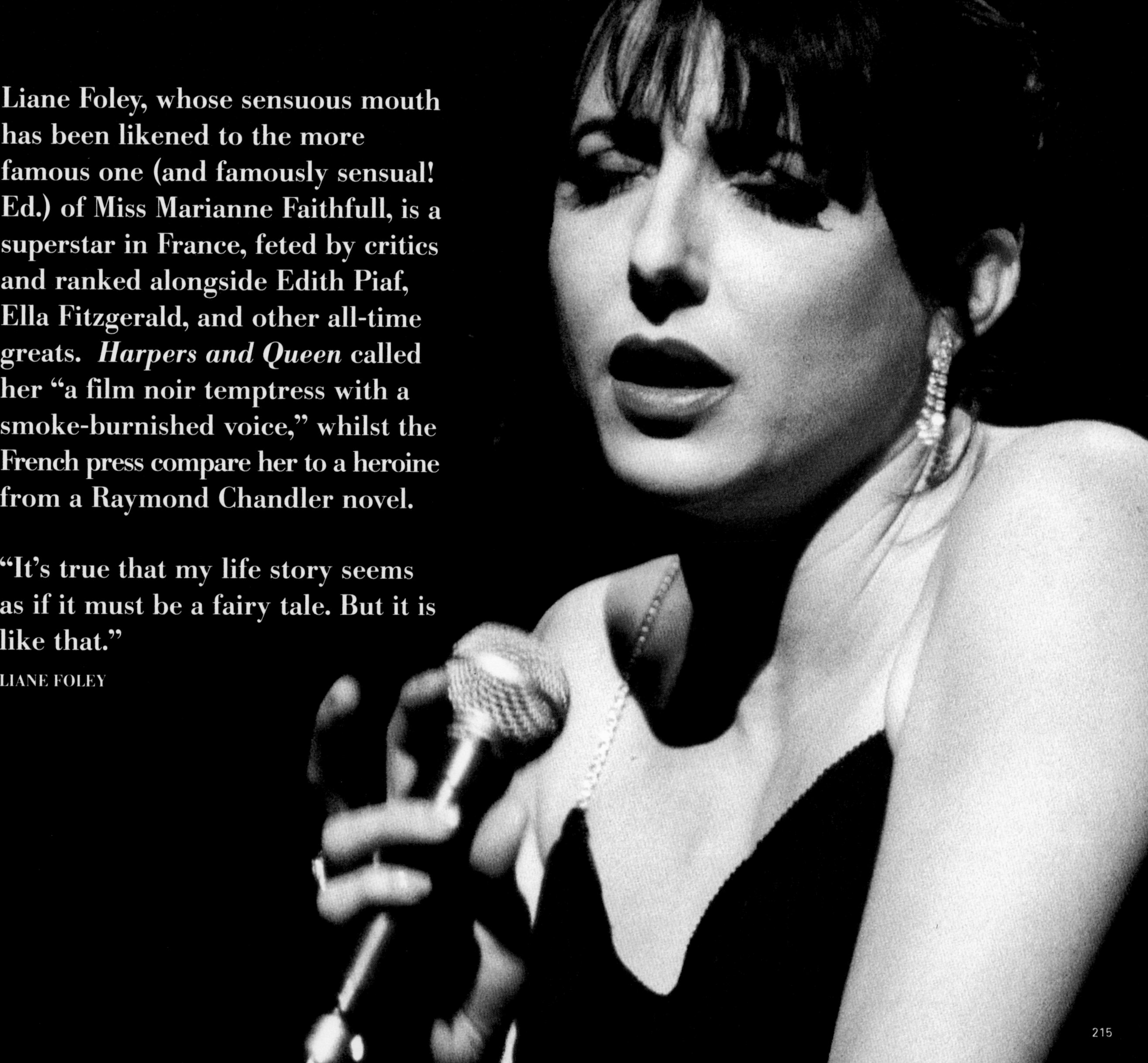

Liane Foley, whose sensuous mouth has been likened to the more famous one (and famously sensual! Ed.) of Miss Marianne Faithfull, is a superstar in France, feted by critics and ranked alongside Edith Piaf, Ella Fitzgerald, and other all-time greats. *Harpers and Queen* called her "a film noir temptress with a smoke-burnished voice," whilst the French press compare her to a heroine from a Raymond Chandler novel.

"It's true that my life story seems as if it must be a fairy tale. But it is like that."

LIANE FOLEY

"...We wanted to make sure that the music had that loose feel, that raw ingredient which TRAFFIC has always had."

STEVE WINWOOD AND JIM CAPALDI

"I'm twenty-seven, I'm married, I've got a wife and kids. How the fuck am I going to play music that says nothing matters? How can I not be fucking **FURIOUS** about the way they're destroying the world my kids have got to grow up in?"

ROB HAGUE, SMASH

"I want it to be the ONLY gig that people would dream of going to, the one they've been waiting for and thinking about."

RICHARD ASHCROFT, VERVE

The gorgeous RuPaul, whom Elton John continues to insist is *"all woman"* and is, according to Stones drummer Charlie Watts, *"too much woman for me,"* is not resting on her well-deserved laurels but is forging ahead with career plans in the U.K. to be announced shortly."

The Auteurs were granted permission to return to their "old school," but "only long enough for one quick pic," said their formally beloved headmaster, who declined to pose with them but has at last apparently dropped all charges.

The music hardly matters, it's just a backdrop to words you should live and die by. Let him take you there.
DAVID GRAY M.M. 3.4.93

"Fantasy-wise, the perfect moment is an autumn afternoon. You're with the woman of your dreams. She's wearing a white dress. You're wearing your best trainers and chasing her around a car park with someone watching."

HOOLIGAN, THESE ANIMAL MEN

Daryll- Ann were at first considered a "novelty group with a novelty name." Under the shrewd stewardship of a certain D. Boyd, Esquire, who "called in a few markers" (to get some arrangements by George Martin, et. el al.), they'd soon gained a very firm foothold indeed in the firmament of megaland. (Let's hope Ken Berry, as is his wont, continues to pay homage where homage is due. Ed.)

acetone

"I'm really looking forward to going out on the road with these songs. They're comfortable keys to sing in, the grooves are mine, and the songs are very much me. That's probably the better part of any vocalist's performance or anybody's work: being in the right place and feeling right about it."

"The score for *The Piano* could get me into trouble. It's a logical extension to my music, but it's also very different from anything else I've done. It's the only time I've ever left a melody alone to breathe its own independent life."
michael nyman

Brian: "We work between the [Alesis] ADAT, the synth gear, and the Apple Mac. A general recording might be put together with live sequences, samples, effects, EQ, etc., recorded down to DAT, then that session might be re-sampled, re-sequenced, or cut up."
Gary: "So we may have a track that we're happy with on DAT. Say it's ten minutes long, but we only want to use the first three. We weld that on to ADAT, resync some [C-Lab] Creator sequences to it, put the next track into [Digidesign] Pro Tools on the Mac, and resync that up to the ADAT, set everything playing, then record it all down to ADAT. We have a professional Sony DAT also synced to the ADAT, so we can throw in stuff from there."
Brian: "This whole image of electronic music being a set of beautiful sounds that you can manipulate — that's not the case. We're great believers in bad-quality samples dictating a mix: a really crackly sample that can only be EQ'd one way, for instance. We'll immediately lop off the top end because the sample has to be like that. Then jam in a nice wide reverb so you've got a depth, a great wafting sound, then you move on. Get a couple of sounds, find some things to fit with it, try EQs and reverbs, and just build up from there."
Gary: "Any systematic way of working, we stand against that. Every time we write anything, we think, 'Well, we've heard it in that, that, that, and that,' and so we try and start again. It's like constantly beating ourselves up. 'Cos what we're trying to do is something that is not only coherent and works, but is extremely different too, and that is fucking difficult."
Brian: "And that's where the visuals come into it. Because, apart from anything else, that's where things are going to go. We might grab a small string sound from a film, reverse it, put it through a reverb, echo, drop it on to DAT, resample it..."
Gary: "...bring it up on the left and right channels on the desk, take the right completely down, force the sound through the delay on one side so it spills over on to the right..."
Brian: "I'm into chaining effects: echo into reverb into something firing off to the side."
Gary: "The Bel delay and Roland Space Echo are useful, and we force things through the ring modulator on the EMS. We'll record things through cassette decks and overload the outputs, then resample it."
Brian: "Something on cassette might be of really shit quality, so you take the filter down and it's muffled, and you work with that."
Gary: "My production strategy is no production strategy. But I think the album has come out sounding very produced, very lush, with plenty of headspace – that's Brian's touch. He's obsessed with making things spin 'round your head. The best thing that I can do with a keyboard is to write an awful sequence – the first thing that comes into my head – find the notes that are going to work, scramble it into the computer, muck around with the editing page until it's vaguely in time, then find a sound on the synth that sounds great. Or we might sit with something like the EMS, get as many sounds out of it as we can, drop them all to DAT, then resample them. Similarly with Indian percussionists and violin players we use: Let them run rampant, then dip into it. When people are given a track to play, they automatically become limited. This abstract, non-linear collage method is a far greater means of expression for me these days."

FUTURE SOUND OF LONDON

"I don't think we're the most talented band in the world. We're not the best musicians in the world, but we do have heart. And I believe if you find the heart of your band, that takes on a power and magic all of its own. You become distinct. You become individual."

Billy Corgan
Smashing Pumpkins

are you
curious about

"The problem with success
is that you don't have time to go fishing."
J. J. CALE

didn't need inspiration to start ıging – I've always sung. I started ıging at three in church. Everybody ɔund me sang. It was just something at everybody did."

hich three crucial books would you commend to the readers of *Straight Chaser*?

Know Why the Caged Bird Sings by aya Angelou, *Disappearing Acts* by rry McMillan, *Joseph & His Brothers* Thomas Mann."

hat's the most spiritually charged place u ever visited?

'ly grandfather's church."

hat's the most negative place?

he Welfare Office."

there one thing you carry with you all e time?

'ep. Love."

CARLENE ANDERSON
STRAIGHT NO CHASER, MAY '94

"Sometimes my own conscious and active 'waiting' is rewarded by an incredible feeling. As if an outside influence has entered me, sound is channeled through my body like a flute; there's no sensation in my throat. What I'm hearing is a better rendition of the song than I could ever have rehearsed, and at that point, I become simply a listener."

SHEILA CHANDRA

"When I was seven years old I was struck down by the musical disease."

GEOFFREY ORYEMA

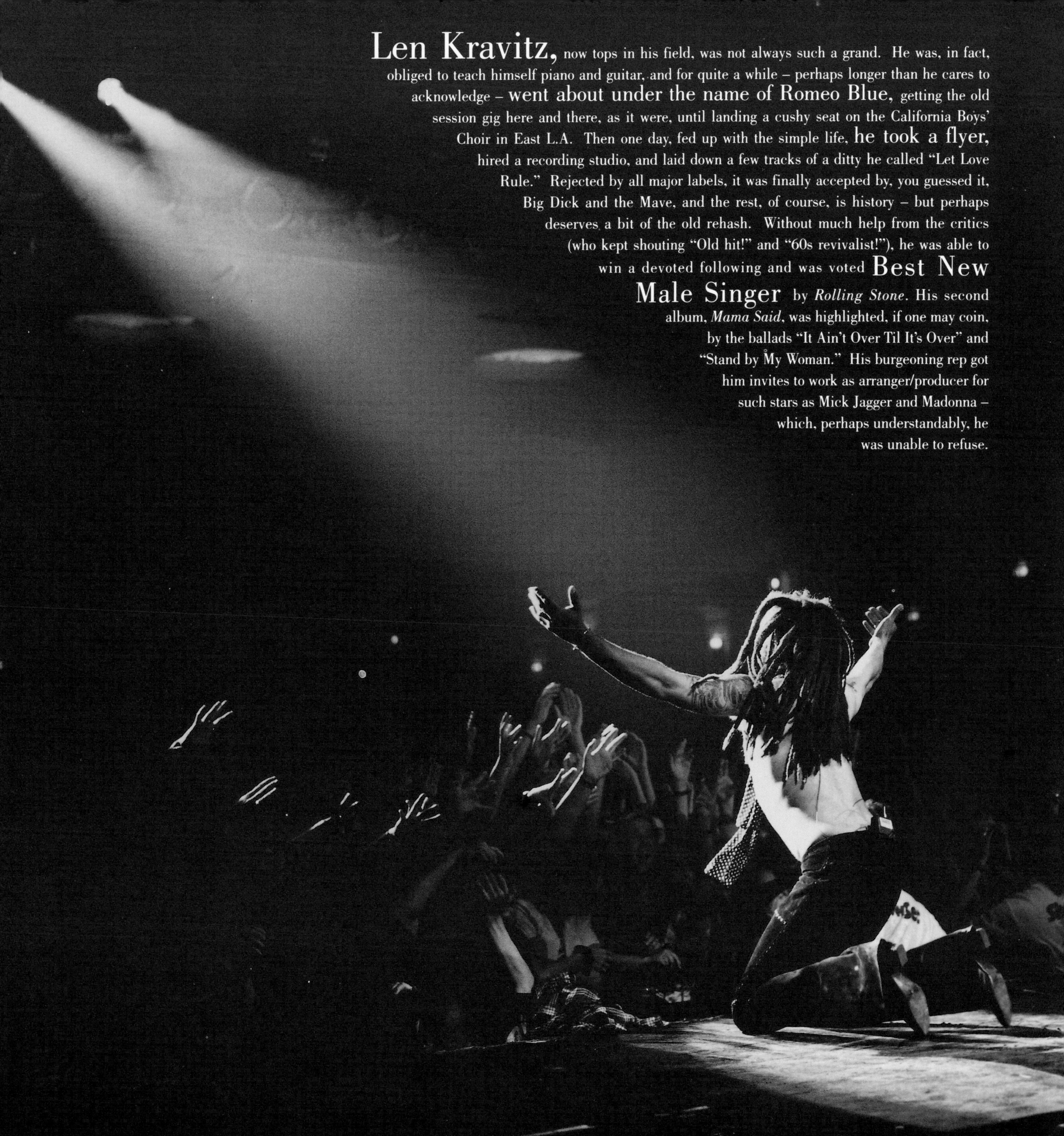

Len Kravitz, now tops in his field, was not always such a grand. He was, in fact, obliged to teach himself piano and guitar, and for quite a while – perhaps longer than he cares to acknowledge – went about under the name of Romeo Blue, getting the old session gig here and there, as it were, until landing a cushy seat on the California Boys' Choir in East L.A. Then one day, fed up with the simple life, he took a flyer, hired a recording studio, and laid down a few tracks of a ditty he called "Let Love Rule." Rejected by all major labels, it was finally accepted by, you guessed it, Big Dick and the Mave, and the rest, of course, is history – but perhaps deserves a bit of the old rehash. Without much help from the critics (who kept shouting "Old hit!" and "60s revivalist!"), he was able to win a devoted following and was voted Best New Male Singer by *Rolling Stone*. His second album, *Mama Said*, was highlighted, if one may coin, by the ballads "It Ain't Over Til It's Over" and "Stand by My Woman." His burgeoning rep got him invites to work as arranger/producer for such stars as Mick Jagger and Madonna – which, perhaps understandably, he was unable to refuse.

"We were playing a festival in Belgium to about 60,000 people - the atmosphere through the whole place was great, but there was this one guy you couldn't help but notice, standing absolutely straight, head and shoulders above everyone else, right at the front, trying to look seriously heavy metal, but with his arms folded, un-moving, face set like the proverbial mask of the grim reaper, absolutely refusing to enjoy a single thing right the way though the whole show. So toward the end of our set I jumped at him so I was literally shouting into his face, 'What's the matter with you, man - I mean, what is the matter?! You *want* to be miserable?!' There was this pause - and not that I'd do it again you understand!, but I found myself looking the guy straight in the eye while the song roared on all around us, and then suddenly his face just cracked into this beautiful, huge grin and he started waving his arms and joining in with the music. Now a cynic might say,'Oh, it was just the attention-' but I actually don't think it was- It was the music and what comes with it anyway that once he let it get to him, simply started to make him feel a whole lot better."

LENNY KRAVITZ

"A tree had fallen on the sign outside the hall and my name was kinda dangling there , **so poetic.** The sound man walked off, a tree had fallen on his house so I guess he decided it wasn't worth doing a sound check. And literally the first two rows were filled and that was it. I was angry and depressed but there was this large, **fat woman,** who must have been 65 years old , in the middle of the front row and it was like **God had put her there.** I played the whole show for her, and then the other 25 people joined her and it was a great show, because she was willing. This was her night out and **god damn it,** she was going to have **a good time."**

LONDON WAINWRIGHT III, 10/89

YES IT'S NUMBER ONE IT'S HOT DINNERS!

FULL STORY INSIDE

HERE IN AMERICA THE
UE BUSTED ONE OF
SUPERGROUPS FOR FOUR
OF L.S.D. HAVING
T THE POSIBILITY OF
UTING IT AMOUNG THE
CAN PEOPLE, NIXON
S TO BLAST IT INTO SPACE
CAPE KENNEDY

MIDNIGHT
OOPS THEY'RE AT IT AGAIN

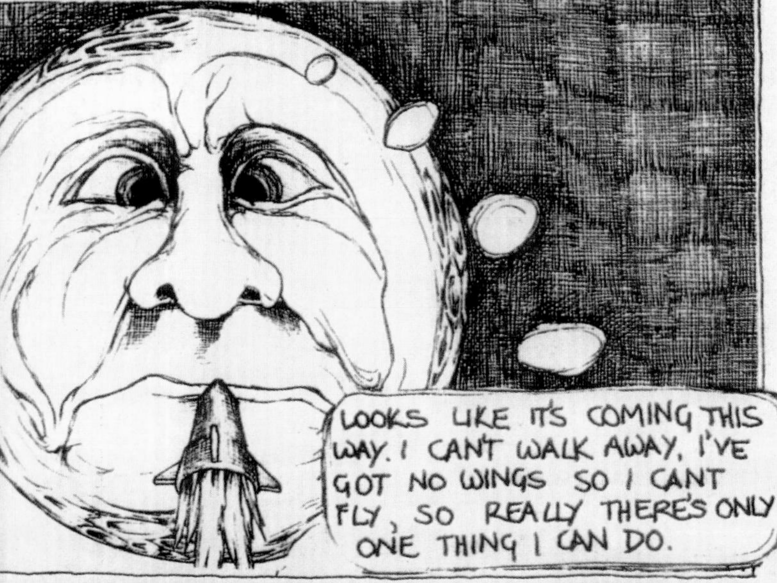
LOOKS LIKE IT'S COMING THIS WAY. I CAN'T WALK AWAY, I'VE GOT NO WINGS SO I CANT FLY, SO REALLY THERE'S ONLY ONE THING I CAN DO.

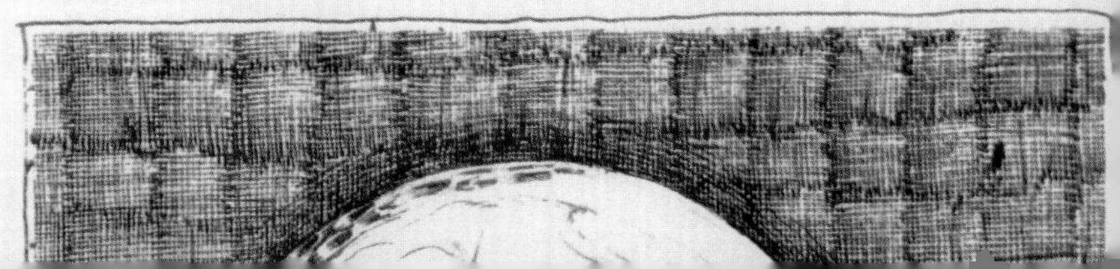

AFTERWORD

BY **SIMON DRAPER**

"I'd just finished my degree in South Africa and was **looking for a decided change of style and pace,** so I moved to London toward the end of 1970. I rented a flat but had very little money, so in the beginning of January '71, I went to see my second cousin, **Richard Branson,** about trying to get a job. I already had a passionate interest in music, so the two things seemed to go very well together. I didn't intend anything other than a short spell working with him, but it turned out to be twenty-one years! Richard's real interest at that time had been in starting a magazine out of which, almost as an aside initially, came the mail order company. That was an inspired concept on two levels: one, because the music it covered was so specifically hip and aimed at albums as opposed to just lightweight singles, and secondly because Virgin provided the best discounted records. Just prior to Virgin's formation, it had actually not been possible to discount records because the re-sale price maintenance meant that you had to sell records at the price set by the manufacturers. That ruling was abolished and initially no one did anything about it until Virgin stepped in to become the first people to start discounting. So, of course, this was spectacular cachet for the mail order business – great selection of records and all discounted – fantastic!

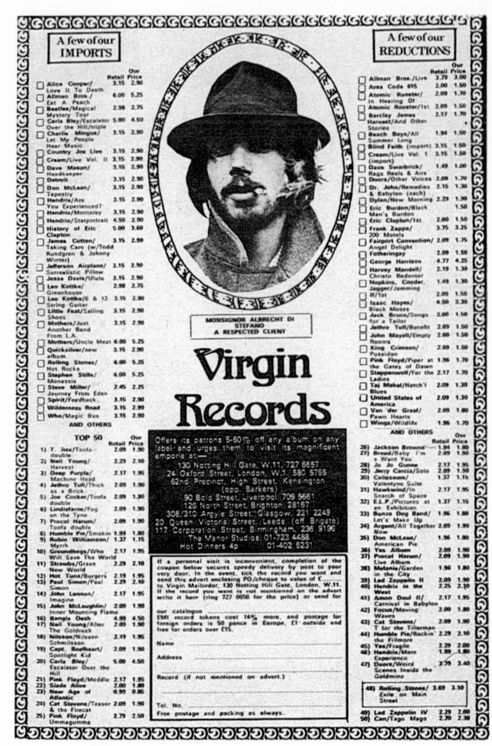

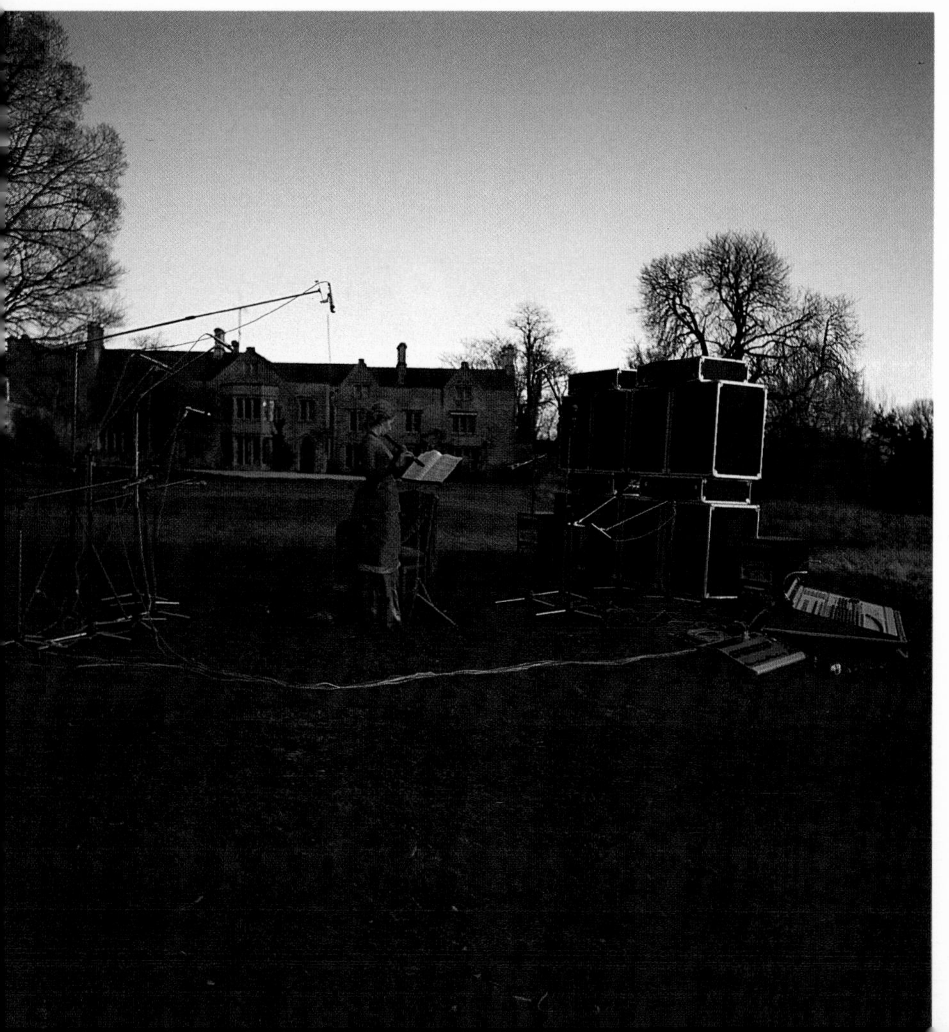

"The first day I started, I remember the mail order company was suffering somewhat due to a postal strike. The first shop was literally just about to open at 24 Oxford Street. I think its opening actually saved Virgin there and then because the postal strike, of course, meant no orders: couldn't post anyone their records, but more importantly, couldn't receive any money.

"That same day that I started, beginning of '71, Richard showed me the designs for the logo which **Roger Dean** had done and talked to me about his plans, which were really quite grandiose. I mean, he'd already bought the manor and was intending to turn it into a recording studio. He was intending to start a management company, a publishing company, a record company, and in fact, within about two years of that date, we'd actually at least started all of those things.

"In the middle of '72 Richard said to me, 'Now we're going to start the record label' - so as I began to look around for artists it came as a bit of a surprise to realise that I wasn't going to be able to sign the kind of music that I was into, which at that time was mainly American - Little Feat, the Band, Captain Beefheart. That sort of music wasn't being made in Britain. What we were already doing, of course, was importing records for our mail order customers that they couldn't get in German and English electronic music, the sort of New European scene, records by Gong, for example, which had previously come out of a small record label in France called B.Y.G. So it became fairly obvious that this was going to be our own special little area to develop. I have to say that although I liked the music, it wasn't what I was really into personally, but **I went ahead and started the record company from this tiny little room above the shop in Notting Hill,** but by the same time we actually launched the label, we'd moved to Vernon's Yard, a mews just off Portobello Road, where we stayed until '84."

KEVIN COYNE
HEARTBURN
KEVIN COYNE · HEARTBURN
Out of the corner of his eye
He saw his death.
And the songs inside his heart
Were glowing coals
That stopped his breath. J.V.
RIGHT
LOOK LEFT
LOOK LEFT
RIGHT
KEVIN COYNE'S NEW ALBUM
OUT NOW ON VIRGIN RECORDS AND TAPES.
V2047.
KEVIN COYNE - HIS MUSIC, HIS WORDS, HIS BAND
April 6 Manchester Umist (Main Theatre, Renold Building), presented in association with Piccadilly Radio.
April 7 Middlesborough Little Theatre, presented in assoc. with Radio Tees.
April 8 Glasgow City Hall, presented in assoc. with Radio Clyde.
April 9 Newcastle University Theatre, presented in assoc. with Metro Radio.
April 10 Edinburgh Music Hall, presented in assoc. with Radio Forth.
April 11 London New London Theatre.
April 18 Nottingham Playhouse, presented in assoc. with Radio Trent.

"In my view, Island were far and away the best record label in the world at the time and was definitely the company we modeled ourselves on. I think that, at a certain point, **Island** became an entirely different sort of company and in the '80s we took off into another area and became a mainstream international competitor with the big corporate companies, but in the '70s we were more alike. I just don't think we did it as well as Island, but then they were already the best. Also, I suppose I did know that to make any impact at all, to have any kind of reason for being, we had to be different, had to find our own niche. So we made records which were, as far as I could do it, very original - very esoteric. Maybe we went too far in that direction with some

tangerine dream

ziggy marley

of the groups, but we were encouraged by the fact that some of those kind of out-of-the-mainstream-type records did extremely well - Tangerine Dream, *Tubular Bells* - to the point where we started to feel that we knew it all, that we were actually **privy to some kind of special knowledge.** Our come-uppance came in the mid-'70s when we found that to survive we had to mature as a label and broaden our roster and somehow avoid disappearing down the blind alley of only pursuing one type of music, one direction. So we spent a lot of energy in '75 trying to sign credible rock acts - still sticking to our principles - we were still very idealistic. We definitely weren't about to completely surrender to commercialism, and it was for that reason that 10 cc would have been such a wonderful signing. It was very disappointing when we didn't get them. We came as close as you can get, but it wasn't to be. Then in '76 we really had to clear the decks. It was extremely difficult, not least because the team I'd built up to work with us on Virgin were all highly motivated, and although I was responsible for all of the signings, it was actually virtually impossible for me to make a signing without getting the support of some of the key people involved. I mean Al Clark, for example, the press officer, worshipped the ground that Ivor Cutler walked on, but we had to make a move. To survive, we had to make a radical change and drop acts who, whilst very good, were never going to improve their sales and become major stars in the mainstream. So we had to clear the decks in order to sign new artists."

mike oldfield

richard branson

"We tried to sign the Stones, Pink Floyd, the Who, but none of them really took us seriously. They were impressed by Richard's boldness in trying to make the big jump, and they were impressed by the fact that we could come up with the money, which Richard did by going 'round and tapping all of the licensees and trying to get a kind of co-operative thing going. But I don't think any of those bands really took us seriously, however, because in spite of Tangerine Dream, *Tubular Bells*, we were still really a very small company at that time.

"Then punk music began to happen in the clubs, and with people making records at home, when it started out it had a life of its own. Record companies were very frightened by it because they didn't have any control over it or any real knowledge of what it meant. Personally, the sort of music I was listening to in '76 was Joni Mitchell, and we'd just done a deal with ECM, the jazz label, so I was submerged in Keith Jarrett's music and all of that stuff. Then out blasts this sound which I suppose was quite similar to music I'd loved in the past – the Velvet Underground, for example – but I didn't want it to be. I didn't like the fact that it existed. I went to see the Sex Pistols and really didn't like it at all. I was very against signing them, which we could have done because Malcolm McLaren offered them to me straightaway. What a mistake, eh?

"A few weeks later, I heard 'Anarchy in the U.K.,' which was clearly an absolute classic, and obviously deeply regretted not having signed them the first time around. Then there was the Grundy episode, where encouraged by Bill Grundy, they uttered a few expletives on live television, and that's when Richard really became aware of them, because they were suddenly so notorious. They were so exciting and absolutely the sort of thing that Richard loves. So he tried to sign them, telephoned EMI, who finally gave them to him, then they signed with A&M, and I think the next day A&M chickened out, which meant finally we were going to get another crack at them."

malcolm mclaren

"**Malcolm McLaren** was very different from any of the other managers around then and probably even now. He was a superior operator really, and he seemed to me to work a kind of permanent revolution system, where whatever anyone's expectations were he would find a way to subvert them, keep people on their toes, make people uneasy. Then Sid Vicious would come around moving from office to office, trying to borrow money from everyone. Although a few people were actually quite frightened by him, basically I think everyone enjoyed working with him because it was just so inspiring. Right from the start the Pistols sold records – not in large quantities though. People often very much overestimate their sales. They sold well in the U.K., but not that much abroad. What they obviously did do, however, was make a huge impact which, of course, was what was important to Virgin at that time.

"Around that same period, I also signed XTC, the Skids, Howard Devoto, Magazine, the Ruts, Penetration ... a long list, because at the same time the music business changed during the mid-'70s and it became no longer possible to easily sell large quantities of albums without having hit singles. This was even more true of most punk rock groups who found it quite difficult to make consistently good albums. So the medium of singles expanded, and because we were heavily committed to this music, we had, for the first time a lot of hit singles – through '77, '78, '79 – and we were very active in trying to work out ways of getting our singles into the charts. So again the company became much more professional, much more mainstream during this time. The snag was that all of the punk groups put together didn't sell as many records as either Tangerine Dream or *Tubular Bells*. Although we'd become much more attractive to a wider range of artists, we were actually not doing so well internationally. This circumstance combined with the recession hitting in 1980 meant that we again experienced exceedingly difficult times. We had **severe cash flow problems** and for the first time really had to look at the bottom line. We were forced to cut the roster, lose staff – which was very painful – and we really had to look to sign bands that as a prime requisite were going to sell records. We simply could no longer afford to be quite so idealistic. So I signed a number of bands at that time who not only turned the company around but also provided, paradoxically, what I think was actually for me the most satisfying and interesting period of Virgin's history."

xtc

"The first three signings that really turned the company into something else were Ian Gillan, Japan, and Phil Collins.

"Ian Gillan came straight in and immediately began to lift us out of the doldrums, move us forward and upward. Japan had a silver record with their first release for us and then gold with their next album.

phil collins

"**Phil Collins** had recorded his album at the townhouse which I'd heard was very good. So I asked to hear it and it was very good! Tony Smith and Phil had decided to sign the record in the U.K. only to either Warners or Virgin, so we **had to fight** quite hard to come up with the deal, which was quite steep actually. But I reasoned that he'd sold records before with Brand X and this record seemed to be something very different. I was decidedly confident we could do well with it actually, and the key to it was **'In the Air Tonight,'** which I found myself playing to people every time I wanted to tell them about our new signing. Then Ahmet Ertegun of Atlantic in the States persuaded Phil to put a different drum pattern on it and suddenly it really started to sound like a single and, of course was a huge success."